This is My Story
This is My Song

Sue Williams

(Shalom 4)

Printed by Kindle Print

Also available on Amazon for Kindle

Cover: Diyan Kantardzhiev

E-mail: diyan@innovation-photography.co.uk

Taken from the original painting by Artist Dawn Fisher

www.dawnfisherart.uk Email: dawn@dawnfisherart.uk

Scripture quotations taken from the New International Version (NIV), Good News Bible and The Message.

All royalties from this book will be donated to the Care Fund at Parklands Church, Swansea.

About the Author

 Sue Williams (aka Mama Sue) is a speaker, hospice chaplaincy volunteer, pastoral worker as well as a quirky and zany creative. She has a heart for people and a fierce love for Jesus that shines through in all that she does. As a widow who has had seasons of caring for loved ones, she has ministered to weary ladies for decades through various means. Whether through speaking at events, hosting her biannual TLC days for ladies or the ministry of Shalom4, her home which provides short term respite, her life is testament to God's amazing grace and compassion that she exudes to all she meets. Sue is mother, step-mother, grandmother and great grandmother. At 73, her vibrance and energy is an inspiration to many, young and old.

Acknowledgements

I would like to thank all those who have been a source of encouragement to me whilst writing this book. I'm sorry it's taken such a time. Thank you too to those who have offered to proofread and all else that the process is to its final stage of completion.

I'm sorry if you haven't got a mention in these pages. You are nevertheless a special friend. You know who you are.

I would particularly like to thank Jane Gregor for editing the contents of my writing, like being given a bag of washing and sending it back to me washed, ironed and neatly folded. What an amazing effort you have made for me to be obedient to what I believe God has asked me to do. Thank you, dear friend, as this has been done so generously by you with no self-gain. My thanks also go to Lisa Higgins for kindly agreeing to read over the final text, to Dawn for her wonderful artwork and Diyan for giving this book its cover. Finally, my thanks to Ann Thomas for her brilliant work in getting the book through the publishing process.

But mostly I want thank God for loving me throughout my life, giving me the most amazing experiences with Him, and for bringing the many wonderful precious people into my life.

CONTENTS

THIS IS MY STORY
THIS IS MY SONG

Blessed Assurance is a well-known Christian hymn. The words were written in 1873 by blind hymn writer Fanny Crosby to music written in 1873 by Phoebe Knapp:

Blessed assurance, Jesus is mine!
O what a foretaste of glory divine!
Heir of salvation, purchase of God,
Born of His Spirit, washed in His blood.

> *This is my story, this is my song,*
> *praising my Saviour all the day long;*
> *this is my story, this is my song,*
> *praising my Saviour all the day long.*

Perfect submission, perfect delight!
Visions of rapture now burst on my sight;
Angels descending bring from above
Echoes of mercy, whispers of love.

Perfect submission, all is at rest!
I in my Saviour am happy and blessed,
Watching and waiting, looking above,
Filled with His goodness, lost in His love.

PREFACE

It's over a decade now since I sensed that God wanted me to write a book. I distinctly remember thinking 'surely not me, Lord!' I didn't do particularly well at school - I had no further education, yet I had the deep sense that He wanted me to 'tell of His wonders'.

I remember Psalm 9, which I was reading, and verses 1 and 2:

I will give thanks to you, Lord, with all my heart; I will tell of all your wonderful deeds. I will be glad and rejoice in you; I will sing the praises of your name, O most High...

I was excited and in awe that I should be writing a book about what God has done for me over three-and-a-half decades of my life. Why hadn't He picked someone who was more eloquent, more educated, more intellectual? I'm afraid I don't have the answer. The fact remains for some strange reason He had picked me.

I remembered many characters in the Bible, like Moses and Isaiah, to name but two. They also had questioned God, insisting He could pick someone more able than themselves, but God wasn't having any of it. He told them that He had chosen them to do the job and He would equip them for the task. This gave me such confidence!

Time has moved on since He first planted the first seed for me to write a book and share all He has done in my life. Recently I felt nudged once again by the Holy Spirit to get 'pen on paper' figuratively speaking - fingers on the keyboard.

The nudge to write this book came in two ways. A young lady was staying at my home and as I was sharing some of the wonders the Lord had done in my life, she said 'You ought to write a book.' I had heard this several times over past years, but this time it was different - I sensed it to be more urgent. I felt that inner conviction that only the Holy Spirit can bring and pondered it deeply in my heart.

Just days later I was having a quiet time and reading the Psalms, and I happened to stumble on Psalm 9, together with footnotes I'd written nearly ten years previously. I checked out the verses in 'The Message Bible', a paraphrased modern version, and read this part of Psalm 9:

I'm thanking you God from a full heart. I'm writing the book of your wonders. I'm whistling, laughing and jumping for joy. I'm singing your song, High God.

I couldn't believe my eyes. This felt like a personal letter from God to me. I quickly responded and said, 'Okay, God, I get the message; I'll write this book and tell of your wonders.' I am still in awe of the way the Lord gets our attention.

It was November 2017 when I was needed to help family in Jersey for a seven-week period. As well as giving support and TLC to my family, I knew there would be some spare time. Then it hit me. *This* was the time to write the book! As soon as I made that decision, past memories began to flood into my mind and I became excited, and with fear and trembling I gingerly began to write my story.

I'm writing in my own style. I'm sure I wouldn't get an 'A' grade, but I felt I wanted to allow the words to flow as if I was sitting with you, sharing my joys and sometimes sorrows in the comfort of your own home. My story isn't so much an autobiography, as a time of sharing.

The road I have trodden has often been a very rough path, dark and threatening to overwhelm me, but it has been laced with times of great joy as God has broken into my life and has done great things for me.

The most amazing people intertwined through my story like threads of gold weaving through my journey - wonderful, inspirational people who have enriched my life in so many ways, bringing me to where I am today. I know you too will be inspired by them as you meet them in these pages.

My purpose in writing this book is that you will be encouraged and maybe even challenged to launch out into the deep, abandoning your comfort zone, setting your sails to new horizons as you embrace the love and provision of Jesus in a way you never thought possible.

I promise you that if you do, you will never be the same…

1

MY STEPPING STONES

Let's start at the very beginning.

It was just after the Second World War when the fortunate men and women who survived came back to their homes to resume their lives, having served their country for some years. Most of them were changed forever by the scenes of devastation they had experienced.

My father, a proud Welshman named Douglas Raynham Watson, was then in his twenties and had served his country in the Army in the Royal Electrical and Mechanical Engineers (REME). He met a beautiful northern lass named Joan Coates whilst stationed in Hull, Yorkshire. They married in Hull in 1946 just after he was demobbed and he took his young bride to the land of his fathers - Wales.

His parents had moved to Swansea. In this typical Welsh family, Joan, his new wife, learnt her wonderful cooking skills and became a good Welsh-Yorkshire housewife. Soon they moved into rooms in a community very near the town centre. A year or so later I was born amid the harsh snows of March 1947. I was known as a 'bulge baby', not for my size but for the influx of babies born in this post-war period. My Yorkshire mother and Welsh father settled well in Wales. My father took up a position as a primary teacher in a school some miles away.

When I was a toddler of thirty months, we moved to a brand-new development. It was one of the first stages of council housing in the east of Swansea. A post-war initiative - estates for tenants to rent. The newly-built houses were offered to teachers, solicitors and other professionals.

These houses were quite luxurious at that time. When I was a baby and toddler we had lived in shared rooms in central Swansea. This must have been so exciting for them, being offered a whole house to themselves! It was a semi-detached house with three bedrooms, a bathroom, dining room, lounge and even a downstairs cloakroom. It even had central heating powered by an open fire. There was a very large garden to cultivate and a brick-built coalhouse and shed. The panoramic views were spectacular with mountains and sea views in the distance.

What a luxury it must have been in those days when many houses still had only outside toilets, and bath times entailed hauling an old tin bath into the kitchen and filling it up from boiling water heated in large pans on an open fire.

As a toddler I was still being bathed in a small tin bath in front of the fire. One day I pulled a pan of hot water over my back causing a nasty scald which meant I needed to be hospitalised. After all these years I can still remember the smell of the gauze dressings soaked in deep yellow Vaseline, that they used for weeks to heal my scalded back.

If that fireplace could talk it could tell some tales. I remember when Mum's diamond engagement ring got thrown into the fire by mistake. To this day I don't know how Mum thrust her bare hand into the fire and retrieved her ring - apparently, she didn't even get singed or burnt!

Toast was often cooked on a long toasting fork and was always delicious when it was browned on the fire, and toasted teacakes were something else. As these were post-war times, they had learnt to be economical with all they had, heating water and toasting on the fire. As we shop today among supermarkets of our choice, it's hard to imagine what it was like for them during the food rationing years between 1940 and July 1954.

We settled in well and just a few years later Mum became pregnant, and my sister was born. I'm not saying I was jealous, but Mum told me my reaction to my new baby sister was to ask them to 'put her in the dustbin'. Poor Hilary! That soon changed as we enjoyed many happy years at number 55 together.

When I reached the age of three, I was sent by my parents to Sunday School. I took to it like a duck to water. It was a local 'high' Anglican church. It was very near a Catholic tradition; probably the only difference was that the Queen was the head of the Church, not the Pope, and that their priests could marry. There was a small community of Anglican nuns living near the church who were part of the church community.

As soon as I was old enough, I went along to the Sunday morning services. It became a way of life for me. As I got older, I attended the evening service also. I always felt such a peace inside the church and knew it was where I belonged.

Back in those days Mum's job was to be at home looking after us children, keeping the house spick and span, providing regular meals and doing endless washing, producing well-laundered clothes. I can remember a cylindrical boiler that fitted beside the sink. Each Monday, regardless of the weather, it was pulled out and our bedding and clothes whirled around, filling the kitchen with steam. When the washing was clean, a mangle was used to wring the clothes which had to be turned by hand. We all helped to hang the washing on the line to dry.

We could hardly contain our excitement when they purchased a twin-tub washing machine that washed the clothes, then you would grab the steaming garment with wooden tongs and plunge it into the spin dryer to rinse and spin. How archaic that sounds now!

My father's teaching post started in a village about seven miles away. He would cycle to work each day come rain or shine. Public transport was difficult from where we lived and cars were for those with lots of money. I recall being told that he occasionally took me with him on the bike. To this day I'm not sure where he put me to sit; probably in a basket in the front: no Health and Safety to consider!

The teaching profession was highly respected and my father loved his role. He managed to get a teaching post in a school within walking distance of our home, which made life somewhat easier without all the travelling.

I began my primary education in Tirdeunaw school followed by Gwyrosydd School - the school Dad taught in. My sister Hilary and I were both very happy there. It was a stone's throw from our home and was so convenient for us all.

Post-war life was bringing so many changes for my parents, least of all the home luxuries that had started flooding into the shops. When we girls finished our infant schooling, Mum decided to go out to work to provide some luxuries for us. Having persuaded Dad, she took a job in the buying office section of a local toy factory where Corgi toy cars were manufactured, and latterly Fisher Price toys also made.

Later in her working life Mum was employed as a receptionist in a local doctor's surgery. She was such an efficient and social person. This type of job was tailor-made for her. We had many extras because of her hard work, such as a television just in time for the 1953 coronation of Queen Elizabeth.

The next big purchase was a car. I remember it was a shiny black car with the registration HI 6890. We felt like princesses going out in it for the first time. Days later it broke down right outside the Civic Centre. I remember the air was blue with the verbal exchange between my parents as they tried to get it going again.

During my second year in the junior section of the local primary school where my father taught, I began to feel quite unwell. I was very tired and felt very sensitive and tearful. This led to many hospital tests. I was diagnosed with a shadow on my lung and mild TB. My main memory of this, besides the awful exhaustion, was having to be built up with a daily drink of raw egg in orange juice: not a pleasant experience.

Within six months I was well again and back into the swing of life. During the time of my illness my parents made the decision that my health was more important than pushing me in education.

The final class in junior school was J4 'scholarship class', which happened to be the class Dad taught. It wasn't always easy to have your dad as your teacher. As soon as I arrived at school, I had to remember to call him 'Sir', a term used in those days for male teachers. Sometimes I forgot to revert back to calling him 'Dad' at the end of school time - inevitably he often got called 'Dad' in school and 'Sir' at home.

The downside of having a father teaching in the same school was if I'd been naughty or made a silly mistake, I would be reminded of it at home and told off again! However, there was one perk and that was to be ink monitor. My task was to fill the ink pots up. This was an important task in those days!

Can you imagine doing that now? It must have been a huge disappointment to him when reading out the passes and failures on the big day of scholarship results and discovering that my name was among the failed pupils.

He was a strict but good teacher, very popular with the parents because he was very fair, and worked hard with those children who struggled but attempted their best.

One of the funny things he did at school which I discovered when I was in his class was his bad habit of smoking a pipe. Every now and again when he set work for us, he would disappear into the storeroom. He thought we were all thinking he was being conscientious by tidying his stockroom. It was years later that I told him that we knew he was puffing away at his pipe! The giveaway sign was the belching cloud of smoke that escaped through the vents into the classroom. I'm not sure how healthy this was for his pupils though. I still have some of his Gold Block brand tobacco tins to this day. They've made excellent containers for my sewing needles and buttons.

My sister Hilary and I enjoyed a secure and happy childhood, with many luxuries that others around us didn't have. We had both sets of grandparents; Mum's parents lived in Hull in Yorkshire and visited us regularly which we always enjoyed.

Dad's parents and sister lived locally so we had regular lovely times with them. My Welsh paternal grandparents and Aunty Betty were strict three-times-on-a-Sunday chapel goers. They had an old organ in their front parlour that needed pumping up. We had many a sing-song as my aunt played and sang hymns as we pumped. Christmas was always fun with them - plenty of love and generosity surrounded us.

I learnt later that Ethel May, my nana as we called her, was a convert from the 1904 Welsh Revival. She was the matriarch of the family, she could be strict, but was kind and loving. Her husband, our Grandpa John Henry, was the most adorable and kind man. Everyone loved this gentleman. I can still see him sitting in his chair in the kitchen with a welcome smile to greet us. Aunty Betty doted on us and we adored going through her beauty cosmetics, perfumes and shoes. What luxury!

We always loved the visits from our maternal grandparents. They would travel by train from Hull in Yorkshire to stay with us; they were well groomed and so much fun. Most of the time we would see Florence, or Florrie as her husband would call her, busily untangling yet another ball of wool, or unpicking an old garment to make something useful for the family; she crocheted too. I still have some of her work. Her baking was wonderful. We loved the days she made bread and we would be allowed to knead a piece to make our own loaf, and oh! the smell of fresh bread cooking wafting from the warm kitchen is etched forever in my memory.

My maternal grandfather, Arthur, we called Pops. Arthur was something else. He was a lovable full-of-fun man. He used to have a horse and cart delivering groceries in the streets of Hull. He liked to gamble and I think often had the wrath of Florrie chasing him. During the First World War in a Somerset hospital he fell, which caused him to lose a leg from the knee down. As children one of the games he let us play was to see how many coins, etc. we could poke down his prothesis so he would rattle as he attempted to walk around. Florrie would laugh helplessly until the tears would roll down her cheeks!

Pops was partial to a drink or two. My childhood memories of him returning with Dad from the local pub was being dropped off by car at the bottom of the garden and him trying to act sober, only to lose his balance because of the artificial leg and end up in one of the rose bushes. We would be watching this from the French window, with Florrie at first fuming that he had drunk too much, then dissolving into uncontrollable laughter that had a way to extinguish any anger she had felt. Happy memories.

2

TEENAGE YEARS

After the summer holidays in 1958, I began secondary education in Mynyddbach, an all-girls school and one of the first comprehensive schools in the area.

I wish I could say I loved my school years, but I hated them. I had no confidence and had a real phobia when it came to tests and exams. I dreaded being singled out in class, to read something out, in case I got it wrong. I stuttered and spluttered my answers. The words seemed to jumble on the page as I went into a near panic attack.

I dragged myself through secondary education, hating every minute of it. I obtained my Swansea Certificate but failed to pass 'O' levels, despite trying my very best. I froze when it came to exams; my mind went blank, then followed panic mode. No matter how much I revised I could not retain what I tried to learn and this has remained a problem all my life. The highlight of that time though was a great bunch of fellow pupils. Nearly sixty years on, some of us still keep in contact.

My teenage years were centred around my local church, St. Albans, and the activities associated with it. I especially loved the Girl Guide movement. I began as a brownie, then progressed to a guide. The practical application of many basic skills we were taught would carry me into my adult life. This was a great opportunity to teach us to become responsible young people. I progressed despite having a fear of exams - the tests and badges we did seemed less daunting.

I became a patrol leader and loved the responsibility the role brought. I even attempted to obtain my Queen's Guide award. Part of my test was to work alongside my local brownie pack. I loved working with younger girls and latterly stood in for our sick Brown Owl. Unfortunately, this meant I could no longer complete my Queen's Guide qualification as I felt the need greater to help keep the pack running.

I eventually took over from dear Mrs Dixon as she was too sick to continue, and remained as Brown Owl for many years, which was hard work, but great fun.

As a teenager, the most important part of my life was my church, and boyfriends which followed a close second!

My church life had started when my parents had me christened at the age of six weeks in St Barnabas Church in the Uplands. My father's denomination was Congregational in an area where my grandparents lived. My mother was of the Anglican tradition. Both hadn't really taken much interest through the war years and in their early marriage.

My church duties as a teenager would include being on the cleaning rota - I can still remember the smell of the wax polish as my dear friend Gill and I would vigorously rub large quantities into the parquet wooden floor in readiness for the polisher. We took pride in our work. When the statues placed around the church got dowdy, we would get out the paints and freshen them up, bringing colour back to them. Nothing too much trouble.

I remember one day Mum being so cross with me and firmly telling me that charity began at home, after she discovered once again the state of my very untidy bedroom. I would leave with no conscience at all to go and clean the church. I could never understand her annoyance at the time, until in later life I too had teenagers!

At one stage when I was about fifteen, I wondered if I should become a nun. God had become special to me. I was in awe of Him but I was just like a grain of sand in the great universe. He was the Great I AM. I knew He was somewhere out there and believed when I prayed to Him that He could hear me, but I didn't think I was important enough for Him to answer personally. He was, after all…unobtainable to us humans…or so I thought.

I continued enjoying each Sunday's services, the pomp and ceremony through the church calendar with its saints' days; through each of the seasons we celebrated in grand style. Youth club and choir were added to my repertoire of church activities and of course the beloved brownie pack and guide company that were part of the church. Friendships of my peers, boys and girls alike, were often from my church community. I particularly liked boyfriends who also loved churchy things too as I would have so much in common with them. Life was full of good wholesome events which I loved.

3

LIFE DECISIONS

Though I had difficulties obtaining qualifications at school, I still desperately wanted to become a nurse. There was a deep sense within me that I knew I would be fulfilling Mum's own wishes for her career. She was unable to do this as her father was so against the idea and it wouldn't have been a popular decision in the 1930s.

During the 1960s it was possible to sit an entrance exam in order to gain access to a nurse training programme by choosing a speciality before training as a qualified nurse.

Mum and I saw an advertisement saying that Winford Orthopaedic Hospital near Bristol was offering places for students to train. I decided to apply. Mum organised the interview and we went to Winford for the necessary entrance exam.

It was years later when 1 learnt that I had in fact failed the entrance exam, but my persuasive mother had pleaded with the matron to take me on: Mum could be a formidable character and she usually got her way!

I had my starting date for the following autumn and would be in residential training for two years. Little did I know that this last Christmas at home before I started my nurse training was going to be a significant juncture in my life.

Our family tradition each Christmas was etched in stone. For me, Christmas celebrations began with

Midnight Mass. Friends and I would wrap up warm and make our way to St Albans Church in readiness to begin festivities. The sense of excitement would heighten as I arrived home to a warm bed knowing that there would be a stocking or two of presents waiting to be opened when I awoke.

Christmas morning was filled with a feeling of love and warmth as we shared our gifts together. Each year Dad would then leave to collect my grandparents and aunt by car after their church service and they would join us.

We would have our wonderfully-cooked Christmas dinner prepared by my parents, and by my sister and me as we grew older. When we had eaten and the washing up finished, tradition would dictate that we all sat for the Queen's speech. No Christmas Day was complete according to my aunt without listening to Her Majesty, much to my father's annoyance who certainly wasn't a royalist. He would then drive them home after an enormous scrumptious tea.

Next day, Boxing Day, we would visit them to let the festivities continue. On the menu for our tea at their home would often be a tin or two of mixed fruit served with bread and butter: a real Welsh tradition. However, this particular Christmas Day was going to be different. Mum had been larking around and caused Dad to twist his neck awkwardly, resulting in him having vertigo, which meant he couldn't drive, so for the first time ever we couldn't visit my grandparents on Boxing Day.

A friend of mine was going to a Christmas party in Swansea and dragged me as a gate-crasher along with her. Here I met Joe who was holding the party at his parents' home. A tall, slim young man who caught my eye and would later become my husband. We began 'courting' and felt even at that young age that we had a future together.

I was still in school studying at that time. I had been accepted to start the nursing course in Bristol the following year, and here I was falling in love with a Yorkshire lad living in Swansea. I should have realised at the time that this would be a great challenge for me.

When it was time for me to leave for Bristol, I was certainly not equipped emotionally. I was inexperienced and left fearful and very insecure.

How different to the teenagers of today; most are quite mature and confident at the age of sixteen. Sadly, within a short time the training proved too much for me. I was terribly homesick and began displaying symptoms of a breakdown. I returned home in a heap. I suppose it was a breakdown of some sort, but with rest and medication I began to slowly improve, but I carried the guilt of failing my parents and myself.

Gradually, I settled back home, enjoying my courting days with my future husband. Mum, in her usually helpful fashion, took charge and organised a job interview for me in the firm she then worked for. I got a job in an office dealing with customers' records and mailing. Years later I took on the job of forms designing.

As was the custom in those days, emphasis was on saving and collecting items for the 'bottom drawer' - a popular custom then for engaged couples preparing for their homemaking. In October 1968 my big day arrived and I married Joe. It was held in the local church that I had loved and attended since I was a toddler. On a misty October day, surrounded by family and friends, I married Joe with all my hopes and dreams ready to unfold. So, a new chapter was about to begin - Sue, a married lady.

After the excitement of the wedding and returning from a honeymoon in Bath, I found it all quite daunting. In those days most young adults, unless they went off to university, didn't leave home until they left to get married. We were quite immature and the thought of leaving and cleaving was quite daunting. With a mortgage to pay, a house to clean and a husband to feed, this was a scary prospect.

I remember our first little house, in the same area as my parents. It was a terraced property, two small reception rooms and a kitchenette with a small lean-to built on. It had the tiniest of bathrooms, and a pretty garden with an added extra outside toilet concealed behind a well-planned mass of perfumed roses. I recall decorating the downstairs rooms with gaudy colours that were popular in the late '60s - bright yellows with shiny navy gloss on the woodwork.

We had been married for over two years, were planning to have a baby and were delighted a few months later when I was pregnant. As I approached the six-week point I suddenly started to have abdominal pain, not severe but enough to know there could be a problem. I remember I'd just finished my brownie pack meeting. I tried not to panic, but later that evening I started to lose blood. Unlike today when an ultrasound scan would be given and your mind would be put to rest, we had to hope and pray everything would settle down and the pregnancy would continue. The doctor's advice was to have complete rest for as long as it took to settle down. I temporarily moved back with my parents, who did an excellent job of looking after me. It took a few months to settle but by the time I was at the six-months stage all was fine, so I returned home and back to a normal life again.

As I drew close to my delivery date, my baby decided to change position and present breech. They tried to turn the baby but it was unsuccessful. Nowadays most ladies would have an elective caesarean section, but I had to try to deliver him 'normally'. It was a traumatic birth requiring forceps and an episiotomy, but it left me torn and very sore.

My baby son was born in a very distressed and shocked state, and was cot-nursed for two days. I wasn't allowed to lift him or nurse him, which was very hard. He kept jumping and seemed very unhappy. When he was allowed to be handled, I tried to breastfeed him myself but unsuccessfully, as he just cried and cried. I reluctantly had to change to bottle feeding. He was so colicky, I even had special medication to put in his feeds and we tried every bottle and teat on the market to try to help, with no change.

The books I had read told me of the wonderful bonding that happened from birth as your baby is placed in your arms, as you fed them and they lay comforted by your presence and body warmth, the sound of your heartbeat, reassuring them of their safety. I had none of that and felt fearful and overwhelmed with inadequacy.

I felt a total failure as a mother as I couldn't comfort my child. This led, I believe, to postnatal depression which is an horrendous thing to have. Following that, I developed obsessive compulsive disorder tendencies which became so crippling. I understand now that it's quite common for this to happen with this type of condition. I would obsess over washing the teats from the baby's bottle, washing them over and over again, then rubbing salt over them, rinsing them again before they went into a sterilising liquid. My hands would be so sore that they would often crack and bleed. The fear of germs led me to sterilise the toys after other children had come to the house and had played with the toys.

At that time the condition wasn't really recognised so the help was limited. Probably most new mums didn't really say anything and I seemed to be surrounded by competent relaxed young mums enjoying their new role in motherhood. I reprimanded myself. Surely, I should be full of joy mothering this beautiful baby boy, who was planned and loved. I had the security of a husband, a home, faithful friends and family. Why couldn't I pull myself together?

As the months moved on, bit-by-bit my confidence grew and as we reached the six months stage my baby was able to cope with food and drink intake without too much suffering. He was covered in eczema which was very distressing for him.

Today I expect he would have been put on a special diet from birth. So much now is understood with postnatal depression and problems with food allergies.

After a few months we decided that perhaps a move might help. I was still a local community girl, but felt the move would be a good plan for our future, so we decided to buy a brand-new house on a new housing estate in the Swansea Valley. It was exciting to watch development as the foundations went up and we saw progress most weeks until completion of our new home. At this time we rented a house for many months on an estate near my parents' home and my church, St. Albans, Treboeth, that I loved so much. I also became a neighbour to a lifelong friend.

At last the day arrived when we could move into our brand-new house. It was built on a private housing estate. We were so excited. It was set away from a main road, towards a small wooded area. It was beautiful - all spanking new and shiny.

There was the local school situated just minutes away with village shops a short walk away. I moved in and soon became part of a community of young parents moving into the newly-built street. I started coffee mornings, joined playgroups and enjoyed the country surroundings that enfolded us. Surely life was going to be perfect...or was it?

My firstborn, was now a strong-willed toddler who stamped his territory straightaway. I'm a bit of an organiser so moving into this new estate where most of the residents were of similar age with young children, they welcomed the social interaction as we acclimatised to our new surroundings.

After just a few weeks I held a coffee morning. I can still remember when, at eighteen months old, my son met his toddler peers as they came to our door and was wielding a big threatening stick at them! One little boy, himself around three years old, was horrified; his enormous blue eyes widened with fear and continued to be very wary of him. I'm pleased to say that 45 years later, even though they both live on different continents, they are indeed still the best of friends!

I found a local Anglican church to attend and got to know many in that community. I went along each Sunday and they became my new church family. I have some happy memories living in Clydach, sprinkled with some quite hair-raising times.

One such instance was at Christmas and I had ordered a new washing machine. Up to that point washing machines were mainly twin tubs. Oh, how I really wanted one of these new automatic machines. I reassured my husband that it would fit into the delegated area in our new shiny kitchen.

He was in work when it was delivered. I remember hastily unpacking it and to my horror finding it just a tad too big to fit in. I was horrified but determined to make it fit. With my husband safely in work, I set about chipping off the plaster with a chisel. To my dismay lumps of plaster began falling off as I got down to the brickwork. I hastily painted the brickwork so it wasn't too conspicuous and gently eased this new 'must have' appliance into its resting place.

For years after, the makeshift wooden fascia I had made to cover up a multitude of sins would suddenly decide to fall off with a loud bang as it hit the floor. But the sound of the swishing water as it went through the cycles and the novelty of putting the dirty washing into the machine and clean clothes coming out ready for drying was a luxury in those days and worth the cosmetic eyesore!

Another memory carved firmly in my mind was of a particularly hair-raising coffee morning. I took my son, then a toddler, across the road to meet other ladies and their pre-school children for a natter and a coffee. We crossed the unmade road and began walking up the drive. To my horror, instead of going for the front door, my son decided to enter the Alsatian dog's kennel with the dog still in it. He didn't seem phased as the dog greeted him with growling and exposing his teeth with anger. Needless to say, it was a heart-stopping moment as we yanked him out backwards until he was safely back in my care. I recovered slowly with a hot strong coffee, only to be traumatised again.

In the afternoon we walked to the baby clinic and he fell backwards onto the unmade road, nearly knocking himself out!

Despite these setbacks we did have some lovely memories in those early years of marriage. But what should have been the happiest time for us had become the saddest. I felt a total failure, very aware of the cracks forming in my marriage. Our marriage had its struggles, but didn't most?

When my son was four years old, I was delighted to be pregnant again and it was unlike the traumatic pregnancy with my son. I remained healthy and gave birth, textbook fashion and full-term, to a beautiful baby girl. How grateful I was.

This time should have been so special, but I was aware of undercurrents in the relationship, sensing my husband's distance, and by the time my baby daughter was six weeks old my whole world fell apart as he no longer wanted to stay with us. After many talks in the following weeks, he decided to stay to give it another go. I was so relieved, but was left with a sense of trauma that affected me for about two years. We humans are very fragile creatures. I felt numbed.

I made many attempts to save my marriage. Some days I thought there was a breakthrough, but other days it seemed hopeless. I remember travelling to London and back on the train for a day trip. One lady in our group looked me up and down and said, 'You are looking well.' She might have meant it to be just that, but I took it that she was saying you are looking...fat.

The very next day I decided to go on a strict diet. I lost a lot of weight very quickly and ended up with anorexia. My doctor insisted on seeing me every week to be weighed. I loved being in a size 10. I would eat my main meal, make an excuse to go to the bathroom, and make myself sick. This went on for months. My body got thinner and thinner but I could only see myself as fat. I'm sure it must have been God's hand on me even then, though I didn't recognise it at the time, but very gradually my mindset started to change and I began to get better.

When I hear today what some poor girls go through, I see I had a very fortunate escape not to suffer for too long with the eating disorder.

I was still attending the local Anglican church. I needed God more than ever in my life, but so often He felt a million miles away.

I began experiencing mood swings, feeling depressed and often overwhelmed with deep inner sadness. I visited my doctor who suggested I began medication to help me through. I was also referred to a psychiatrist and later a psychoanalyst to unravel my emotions and feelings to try to help me through this dark time. I loved attending these sessions as I had someone to listen and help me.

I contemplated suicide. I didn't realise what a self-righteous person I was until I planned a way that would keep my reputation as the 'nice girl' from the estate by the woods who ran the local brownie pack. Little did I know that this time was a crucial plan in my life by God to bring me to Himself.

My Welsh grandmother, Ethel May, whom I called 'Nana', lived nearby in an old terraced house called Peniel Green. 'Peniel' means the face of God. When I was two-and-a-half I was taken there for my heavily-pregnant mum, who had gone into labour, to go into hospital to deliver my baby sister, Hilary.

Not long after I arrived, I fell up the stone step that led into the hallway and was badly cut above my right eye. My poor father had to promptly come back to take me to the doctor for stitching. He used to recall the story and his anger as he held me down to be stitched with no anaesthetic to numb the pain.

To this day I still have the scar to prove it. I'm happy to say that that very stone step became the platform for Hilary and me to perform many a concert, to the delight of the family as they cheered our efforts.

I remember many good times of visiting my lovely gentle grandpa, John Henry Watson, my Nana Watson, who could sometimes be strict with us, and my aunt, who always seemed to have lovely perfumes stored in her bedroom with so many pairs of shoes; it was a delight as a child to be allowed in her bedroom to experience the aromas of her perfumes and try on her shoes.

As a child into my teenage years we enjoyed our regular visits - the glorious wafting cooking delights coming from the old-fashioned kitchen. The walk-in whitewashed pantry that still had the hooks in the ceiling where their predecessors would cure the pigs salted and prepared over the years. The cold slab was full to the brim of tinned products, just in case there were shortages - a throwback to wartime experience.

I especially remember the smell of the pine tree laden with pretty lights and ornaments and the special small Boxing Day gifts especially chosen for all my family.

The front room, formally known as 'the parlour', housed a wonderful organ, with all the stops and pedals to either make a delightful sound or the most hideous! Before I was born, they would gather around this magnificent organ and sing hymns together, which must have been quite something to any passer-by. Hilary and I were allowed to go in to 'play' the organ. I'm sure the sounds were not at all melodious; nevertheless, we were always commended for our music.

My children loved going there, particularly to dress up with the various hats and sticks, and they would strut out proudly to perform to the sound of applause and approving laughter. Over the years many children visited their home and carried on the tradition of stone step concerts!

Some years later Aunty Betty became ill and was taken in for an emergency operation. She had ovarian cancer that had burst. After her operation she was on medication and amazingly never had any further recurrences of cancer and lived to a good age.

When Ethel May Watson, known to me as Nana Watson, was coming to the end of her long and happy life, she had been very unwell and was extremely weak and frail. She was beautifully nursed at home by her devoted daughter, Aunty Betty. As I have said, Ethel May had found faith in Jesus during the 1904 Welsh Revival. Her husband John Henry and daughter Sheila Elizabeth, whom we knew as Aunty Betty, had also become committed Christians.

My means of transport in those days was a Camino moped. You'd turn the pedals to start it off and I chugged along at the top speed of 30mph unless I was going down a hill! When it rained, which was often here in Wales, I had to take off the spark plug, dry it, sandpaper it, replace it and hope that the fresh connection would cause it to fire so that I could go on my way.

I set off on a cold December morning to visit my ailing nana. On my journey to her home, a very strange thing happened. I heard a gentle voice in my head saying, 'Tell Betty to read out loud the Lord's Prayer.' To this day I don't know why I didn't question or analyse the voice. I arrived at Nana's home and told Aunty Betty what had happened. Without question she began to say out loud the Lord's prayer:

Our Father, which art in heaven, hallowed be Thy Name.
Thy Kingdom come. Thy will be done on earth, as it is in heaven.
Give us this day our daily bread *and forgive us our trespasses,*
As we forgive those who trespass against us.
And lead us not into temptation, but deliver us from

evil.
For thine is the kingdom, the power, and the glory,
For ever and ever. Amen.

When my aunt got to the part where it says, *Forgive those who trespass against us*, she broke down crying and asked God to forgive her for a fall-out she had with my mother. She knew God had forgiven her and was at peace once again. Nana, who was asleep in the bed in the parlour, very frail and ready to meet her Maker, knew nothing of the discord between the sisters-in-law. What was quite amazing just hours after my aunt's repenting prayer, my nana slipped quietly away into the arms of her Maker. It was as if she hung on until this had taken place and they were at peace.

Absent from the body, present with the Lord. Ethel May Watson, December 2nd, 1981.

4

A NEW HEART

Here began an eleven-month intense journey which took me to the end of myself as I knew it; to a place that would change my life forever.

I was now aware of what seemed like a tug of war for my soul. I'd never doubted there was a God but I began to wonder if all this was just a nice story. I'd lived a morally good life and as I said earlier, I was very self-righteous. I still loved going to church but I wondered if it was out of habit and sheer routine. Yet at the same time I felt a deep drawing in the very core of my being, a need that I'd never really felt before. I was aware of a chasm within me feeling absolutely empty, almost unbearable.

I often remembered the voice I had heard that day during my bike journey to my nana's home. Why had God spoken so clearly and given me that instruction to give my aunt? How didn't she question it? It all didn't make sense. This was the time that I was being psychoanalysed - maybe I was suffering from a mental illness and was hearing voices and it wasn't God after all. I was in a turmoil and felt the inner struggle like a tug of war between good and evil.

My husband suggested I spoke to a retired specialist who had to retire early due to issues with his health. I was taken to the local pub one Sunday evening and left in a secluded corner with the ex-specialist to discuss my medical issues. How very unconventional!

I sat down feeling somewhat awkward and a bit unsure of this man I hardly knew. He looked at me strangely and said, almost surprised at the words coming out, 'I had to go to chapel for you today and God gave me two words, menstruation and thyroid.' I wanted to run out of the pub, I felt awkward and wondered if this man had had too much to drink! I hastily added that my menstrual cycle was fine, thank you very much. He drew me to the second word - thyroid. He asked if I'd had a thyroid profile done. I said I hadn't. He suggested I went to my GP and ask him to have a blood test to check my thyroid levels. Forty-eight hours after this meeting, I arrived in my doctor's surgery asking him for this test. He readily agreed. The results came back to say I had an overactive thyroid gland.

Why is this so relevant, you may be thinking? For many months I had been treated with antidepressants, etc., and having regular visits as an outpatient to a psychiatric hospital to see the psychoanalyst, when in fact all the symptoms I had were from a different cause. My mood swings and sadness alongside other symptoms were in fact not depression but the effect of an untreated overactive thyroid. I was immediately taken off all medication for depression and started on medication for my thyroid problem.

In a very short time I felt so different and as if I was back to myself again. I began to see these 'coincidences' as what I now know as 'God-instances'. I reflected on the chain of events and it was as if the good side was winning over the evil side.

It was during this time that I was drawn to a group of people in my church. They were dynamic and authentic about their faith; they seemed joyful and at peace in their lives. They met together during the week as a house-group to sing and pray, to read the Bible and talk about God. One Sunday after church they asked if they could pray for me, telling me that being a good person, even though I had been christened and confirmed in my denomination, still didn't make me a Christian. I was shocked at this. They continued to say that I needed to ask God to forgive all my sins and ask Jesus to come into my heart and that then I would know Jesus as my own personal Saviour.

I remember going to bed that night on August 12th, 1982 at thirty-five years old. I thought hard over what they had said and felt I had nothing to lose. So, I simply prayed that very prayer they had suggested and settled down for a good night's sleep. I meant all I said, but I was totally unprepared for what was to happen next.

The following morning when I woke up, to my absolute shock I was totally changed! The first thing I noticed was I felt as if I had been scrubbed on the inside and felt squeaky clean. The peace and joy that flooded my heart was indescribable. I felt I had come alive for the first time ever. Even colours were different! It was as if I'd only ever seen colour in faded shades: they were now vibrant and bright.

All these things were amazing, but the most wonderful was that Jesus had become real to me.

He was now MY personal Saviour, as the Bible describes in John 3:3 where Jesus replied, *Very truly I tell you, no one can see the kingdom of God unless they are born again.* He had washed away my sins. I was a new creation - redeemed, rescued, and I had eternal life.

I understood for the first time what that little group of joyful Christians at church had been sharing all those months. It was like the veil had been lifted and now I could see clearly. The empty chasm deep in my inner being that I now recognised as 'God spot' had been filled by Jesus, my Saviour! I could hardly contain myself. I wanted to jump on a soapbox in a superstore and tell everyone about the love of Jesus that could set them free.

I shared this experience I had with my friends at church who had been praying for me. They of course were delighted, telling me they would nurture me through this new spiritual birth. This was all new to me. I hadn't read books about spiritual new birth so I was eager to understand, learn and grow.

That weekend it was my youngest niece Laura's birthday party. I had taken the children to her party. In those days they were a lot different to the sophisticated parties that youngsters now have: jelly and blancmange and cake was the style. The children all sat around the table and their parents stood behind them talking over their heads as they enjoyed the party food. One lady asked a question to another saying, 'Are you taking your children to Sunday School tomorrow?' 'Yes,' she said disinterestedly, and carried on her sentence 'Same old stuff!'

Suddenly a voice inside me said, 'Tell them to listen to the words.' I felt fearful and silently said in my mind, 'Oh, I can't do that!' Immediately this wafting awesome peace inside started to wane and I instinctively knew I had disobeyed God. I felt bereft and longed to get home so that I could run into the privacy of my own space and talk to God and say how sorry I was. When I arrived home, I went into my bedroom and repented to God for refusing His request, and promised Him I would never do that again and would always speak to anyone if and when He gave me the opportunity. To my great relief His wonderful peace returned to me.

I will never forget the week that followed. Mark, one of my church gang, had pinned an owl badge on my coat with these words written on it, 'Know Jesus, know peace'. I still marvelled at what happened that week. It was as if it became a magnet for everyone I came into contact with to ask what the words on the badge meant.

As I was going into the bank that Monday morning, a lady spotted my badge and asked me. In fact, all week the scene was repeated each day. It didn't take me long to realise that this was God taking me at my word that I had promised Him just days before. I began praying for certain people who were on my heart.

One family I was particularly fond of worked in the village creating lovely items using a pyrography pen, finely burning designs onto wooden objects they had made. They also carved the most beautiful love spoons - carving from one piece of wood then burning designs and bespoke wording onto the creations. This dear family became top of my 'hit list' of prayer for many years. I also had the privilege of working with them selling their beautiful creations and I also had the chance to talk about Jesus.

During that week I was in awe of the freedom and love I felt for my Saviour. As I read the Bible it became alive to me. The same words I had read before had changed from being just words and now became like spiritual food for my soul. I was truly a new person, born again by the Spirit of God. I understood for the first time what it meant to have the Holy Spirit indwelling me. I was also acutely aware that I had a strange physical twinge deep in my tummy that I had put down to excitement from this awesome new spiritual experience.

Just a week after my spiritual awakening I was getting ready for bed, tucked myself in and was reading a book written by Christian author, Colin Urquart, entitled *Anything You Ask in My Name*. I was reading the chapter on healing, and in my mind's eye I saw a gentleman, the retired specialist battling with alcoholism who previously had been used by God to get me to my GP to help me get the right diagnosis of an overactive thyroid. Immediately I saw him in my mind's eye with a glass of orange in his hand and a beaming smile.

As this thought enveloped my mind, I experienced something that was way beyond anything I could have imagined on this earth. The twitch in the centre of my tummy I had been experiencing all week suddenly felt as if it burst open and my very being felt it was electrified. It was as if every cell pulsating in my body and blood was being filled with power. I was lying on my bed, my husband fast asleep beside me. The next thing I knew I felt as if I was coming out of my body and was looking down on myself. I have to admit to feeling very frightened. I had never had anything happen like this before. The pulsating, ecstatic feeling continued and I was aware that there was a Holy Presence above me. I couldn't see anything, but I had a sense I was being drawn towards Him.

I was lost in time and wonder, not wanting it to end

or to be separated from the tangible presence of God. I knew I was being freed from a great fear - the fear of death. I didn't understand at the time the importance of this, but all would be revealed in His time. I was then aware of gently coming back into my body. I didn't want it to end; I wanted to stay in this state but knew that God had a plan for me still on this earth to do. The sensation began to subside as I drew back into my body, back to my bed. I lay there in disbelief at what I had experienced. Yet I couldn't deny any part of it. It had happened. Somehow, I managed to drift off to sleep with the memory etched forever on my mind.

I woke next morning still very much aware of what had happened. I noticed that the palms of my hands still had the same burning sensation as the night before during the out-of-body experience. My hands continued to have immense heat radiating from them and this lasted for weeks.

Because I was very wary of anything supernatural, I wanted to share this experience with a trusted friend and vicar, Rev. Douglas Davies, who had been so much a part of my life since teenage days. I visited him just days after the experience as I was unsure what all this was about as I hadn't read any books of Christians experiencing the power of God. He listened intently as I shared what had happened to me. He gently assured me that it was a very precious experience that God had given me, like an anchor. He also gave me the Scripture from Ephesians 1, which he felt was what God had graced me with in my recent experience: sealed by the Spirit of God - filled with the Spirit of God. What an awesome privilege. Ephesians 1:13:

And you also were included in Christ when you

heard the message of truth, the gospel of your salvation. When you believed, you were marked in him with a seal, the promised Holy Spirit (NIV).

I remember that very soon after this spiritual experience, I had one of our coffee mornings. Most times there would be at least six of us, but this particular time, just two of them, Babs and Mags, turned up. Babs came early; I opened the door and she took one look at me and said, 'Something has happened to you!' She knew things were very difficult in my marriage and laughingly commented had I found a man on a white charger?

I hoped she would drop the subject as I hastily directed them into the lounge while I made the coffee in the kitchen. I returned with steaming coffee for the three of us. Within seconds Babs inquisitively took up the same conversation. 'Well, what's happened to you; have you found another man?' I gulped, remembering my promise to God just a few weeks ago, so I had no choice but to tell them the story of what had happened to me. They listened intently as I shared that I was now a born-again, that Jesus had come into my life and I was heaven bound.

They both said they thought I already was a Christian because I'd been christened and confirmed, I did good works and was a moral, righteous person. I told them I also thought I had my ticket to heaven, but now knew that following all the traditions, doing religious ceremonies, attending church regularly, being good and all that entails just wasn't enough.

A regenerated spirit was needed and to get that I had to be sorry for my sins, ask forgiveness and invite Jesus to come into my life to be my Lord and Saviour as I surrendered my life to Him. All they kept saying was that I looked so different. The sadness of my unhappy marriage had taken its toll, but now I was rejuvenated and full of hope. They left amazed at all I shared.

The following week Babs invited me to her home and we talked for hours as she ploughed through her mountain of ironing. She asked me lots of questions about God, but when I mentioned Jesus as a personal Saviour and even friend, she got cross with me to the point she said pointedly to me, 'I don't mind you talking about God, but I'm uncomfortable with the way you talk about Jesus.' She added that maybe I should leave if I continued, and that she would never talk about Jesus as I did.

Just days later, over the same ironing board, the veil was lifted and her spiritual eyes were opened! She too began a new dynamic, exciting spiritual journey.

In the months that followed I learned more about this new life in Christ and how prayer wasn't a boring exercise but a dynamic communication with God through His Son, Jesus. I had always prayed to God but this was somehow different and it was most exciting to begin to see answers to our prayers as never before.

I mentioned earlier that I had always found school hard. I had difficulty retaining information. This contributed to what I believe was an inferiority complex. I was always frightened to have a go in case I made a mistake. I wasn't confident about much at all really, but I began to notice after this awesome experience with God that this had changed. I felt totally confident. My lack of academic qualifications had always made me feel very inferior: now that didn't seem to matter anymore.

I remember expressing in written words to my parents as a declaration to what Jesus had done for me and could for them also if they followed His Way. My father, who you will remember from earlier, taught me at primary school, had difficulty believing that I'd actually written this myself and was astounded at my wording and creativity through it. God makes us brand spanking new!

One night about six months later I had gone to bed, with my husband sleeping beside me. I went straight to sleep, waking suddenly at 3a.m. to the sound of my name being called: 'Sue.' I was surprised to be as fresh as a daisy which certainly isn't me in the middle of the night.

I left the bed with my husband fast asleep and went into the children's bedrooms to see if they'd called me. They were also sound asleep and I thought how silly of me - they would call me 'Mum'. I concluded it must have been a dream and went back to bed. I snuggled down and started to drift off to sleep again. In the stillness of the silence of night again I heard my name called. I repeated the steps I had just taken. My husband and children were still sound asleep. Too much cheese for supper, I thought, and settled down again. Then louder and more persistent I heard my name being called, 'Sue.' I started to shake as I knew it was a voice I had heard. Was this the same voice I had heard when my Nana was almost leaving this earth?

I got up from bed grabbing my Good News Bible. I took it downstairs with my body shaking. I sat down and opened my Bible at random. It opened on Isaiah 43. I started to read the first few verses which said:

Israel, the LORD who created you says, 'Do not be afraid - I will save you. I have called you by name - you are mine. When you pass through deep waters, I will be with you; your troubles will not overwhelm you. When you pass through fire, you will not be burnt; the hard trials that come will not hurt you.'

How could the God of the universe call me by name and lead me to this very Scripture? This was the prompting of the Holy Spirit. He was saying something very specific to me. I was His, I was safe, I didn't have to be afraid because He would be with me. I had no idea at the time how prophetic that Scripture would be for me and a vital anchor to bring me safely through the years to come.

There is a 'gospel' out there suggesting 'Come to Jesus and everything will always be fine'. It is not true. What He promised isn't a life of roses, but through every circumstance that comes our way He would be closer than the air we breathe.

This is my experience throughout my journey to date. I didn't always get things right and made some big mistakes on the way but I knew the forgiveness that Jesus offered when I was truly sorry.

Despite my wonderful spiritual experience, my home life got increasingly difficult. I have to say it must have been a shock to my family. They were pleased that my health issues had improved but my new-found commitment to Jesus was bewildering, especially to my husband. I was so passionate and enthusiastic about my new life in Christ that it became a threat. I wasn't always very wise in the way I handled things. It was like living in two worlds.

I found my interest in secular things dwindled as more and more I began to learn the ways of becoming a true disciple of Christ and what this meant in everyday life. In hindsight I probably would have done things differently but I did what I felt was right at the time.

Consequently, my husband put restrictions on me seeing some of my Christian friends, especially those who held beliefs like mine. He wanted me to become a 'normal' Christian again instead of the born-again Christian I had become.

It was tough to say the least. To keep his memory dignified I have decided not to go into details about his life issues. It was a very sad time as I saw his health deteriorating because of his issues. Our children loved him dearly and he was a dedicated and loving father.

5

DREAMS AND VISIONS

I don't dream much, but I knew at the time that this was so different and has been imprinted in my spirit; even after all these years it has left, and still does leave, such an impression on me. At the time I was attending a typical Anglican church and was still very traditional in my taste of worship, etc.

In my dream I was aware of standing in a long queue outside what appeared to be a really ramshackled tin-type building, so very different from the type of church building that I was used to. I appeared to be with friends, the sun was shining and I felt warmed by the rays.

We were happy, relaxed and full of anticipation in readiness for the church service that was going to take place. The doors were opened and we all filed inside the building, which was two-tiered. I went upstairs and sat in the middle of the front row of a balcony.

As was then my tradition, I went to kneel and pray as I settled into my seat. I was aware of the sun pouring through the windows, which brought both warmth and awareness of thousands of dust particles dancing in the air as the rays hit each one. As I knelt down, I was aware of thick dust layered on the floor, so I folded a cloth on the floor and knelt on that so that I didn't get dirty. I sat back in my seat. I was aware of those in the downstairs section - they appeared to be unkempt, like tramps, and were seated in a semi-circle and had what appeared to be large enamel bowls upon their laps.

The service started, gutsy heartfelt singing coming from those on the balcony, then the minister or vicar, standing on the left side of the staircase joining the two floors, started to pray. I shut my eyes, absorbing the warmth of the sun and the contents of his prayers; his prayer language changed from English to another tongue; I knew this was OK and scriptural. I felt safe and although I couldn't understand him in the logic, I did understand what he was saying in my spirit (hard to understand, I know).

I could feel warmth rising upon me and filling me with overwhelming joy and peace; my eyes were still shut. As I bathed in what I believed was His presence, I became aware of the voices getting distant, the air becoming more chilly and I was rising up and being taken somewhere else…bleak…it felt like a place that was cold, desolate and barren, my eyes were still shut…but I still felt safe; I could hear a noise, a thud… then again, another thud…it was getting louder…I heard **that** cry…I 'felt' the pain **and knew** without seeing that the thuds I had heard, and that awful cry, were the nails being hammered into the hands of my Saviour Jesus and His anguished cry of terrible pain.

I cannot describe the pain I felt. I sobbed and sobbed with conviction of what my sin and the sin of others had cost Him…the depth of pain He must have felt was unbearable…He was carrying my sin…and the sins of the world…I don't know how long I was there…time was not in the equation…then I became aware of singing voices faintly in the background, the chilliness was being replaced by the warmth of the sun once again. I was aware of being transported back to the ramshackled building with its dirt and dust and tramps. But as I opened my eyes I had not been taken back to my seat on the balcony, but was downstairs amongst the 'tramps'; they were saying 'sick sick' and I found myself in the front of this building as if in front of an altar, on my face on the floor before the Lord, sobbing and pleading for those who were begging for help.

I woke, my face wet with the tears I had shed, deeply affected by what had happened, knowing this was no dream...I knew deep within the core of my being what God was showing me: I would have avoided 'germs'. Over the years I have been quite phobic about 'catching' things. I was 'self-righteous' and proper, and worshipped Him on my conditions and within my comfort zone.

I knew this to be my challenge, my commission, my opportunity to obey and serve my Master. He was taking me out of my comfort zone and wanted me to get amongst those who would cry, 'sick sick.' Some would be physically sick, others would be spiritually sick, and as those He would entrust to me, I was to take them, pray for them, love them and plead for them before the altar of God, before the cross of Jesus. I was to walk with them, hold their dirty, smelly, sin-diseased, soaked hands and love them as He did.

Over the years I have had the privilege of doing this and will share them with you in subsequent chapters.

All through my life I had always stayed clear of any supernatural phenomenon. This new way of living as a committed Christian clearly involved the supernatural but I could see as I checked in the Bible which were God's supernatural ways and which were of Satan.

In the early days of being a follower of Jesus, I remember coming into the understanding of the gifts of the Spirit. I prayed and thanked Him, asking Him for all the gifts He wanted to bestow on me...except for one particular one. This was the gift of tongues. I had a fear that it would take me over, possess me. Perhaps it showed a lack of trust in God, for He says He will give us no bad gift, but I still didn't want it.

Some months later I remember vividly, as I vacuumed the carpets at home, that I was overwhelmed with praise for this God who had sent His only Son to die on the cross for me to be set free. I was almost running out of words. Quite spontaneously I started singing in gratitude and love for Him, then realised I was not singing in English but in a foreign language that I didn't understand; yet deep in my spirit it seemed to make sense and filled me with supernatural peace.

So great was His love for me that just like a gentle father He brought to me the gift of tongues that I so ungraciously was opposed to receiving from Him. I soon learned that this very gift was such a source of power when praying, especially in spiritual warfare that the words, unknown to me, were Holy Spirit-led and would personally edify me and could be used in my own devotional time. At church occasionally I would hear someone bringing a message in another tongue which would then be interpreted by another person to build up the church.

One evening sometime later I had a call from a neighbour: she and her husband were Christian friends of mine. Hazel rang to ask if I would call in that evening to pray for her husband, Mark. I said I would and asked God to show me how to pray for him. He said, 'pray in tongues.' I thought, 'Oh no, I can't do that!' One reason was that I had never prayed out loud in tongues and I supposed I felt very self-conscious. The other reason was that I knew Mark had so desired the gift of tongues and it had never been given to him, and here I was not wanting it and it was given to me! I went in that evening in fear and trembling.

I shared what I felt God had asked and Mark humbly accepted and encouraged me to pray just as God had shown me. A big gulp, and I hurriedly spoke out in tongues, completely out of my comfort zone and to be honest was glad when I finished. Mark sat there with a big beaming smile on his face. I looked at Hazel who asked Mark if he was okay. Mark nodded contentedly. He wrote some words in a notebook and said he was fine, but he couldn't speak at all. I was so uneasy but he reassured me as he continued to communicate with his notebook and pen.

I went home very unsure and wondered what I had done. I called there early the next morning. I was greeted by his wife Hazel who said he still couldn't speak, but was fine. Hazel had to ring his place of work to say he couldn't get to work because He had lost his voice, which of course was true; I think they may have thought he had laryngitis! A few minutes later, Sarah, their toddler daughter of eighteen months, had got hold of a steel knitting needle and was making a beeline for the 13amp electric socket. Mark stood up to warn her and with that his voice returned as the protective loving father called out her name urgently to save her from what could have been a fatal accident.

To this day we never did understand the purpose of God taking Mark's voice for nearly twelve hours.

Unknown to me when I went in that evening, just hours before I got there, Mark was reading this passage of Scripture, Ezekiel 3:26:

And I will make your tongue cleave to the roof of your mouth, that you will be dumb...

You can imagine my amazement to hear this. Mark said he had a precious little time writing down all God was showing him, and Hazel had no choice but to lead their bedtime Bible study for the first time as she had never felt confident before.

His ways are certainly not ours. He showed His power to us that evening in a way that was beyond our understanding. We were in awe of our mighty Lord.

6

I AM WITH YOU

The tensions continued to grow at home and came to such a pitch that my praying friends sent up an SOS prayer for help. They asked God to answer within 48 hours as they were so worried about me. The following day I was scheduled to look after Les's son while she went to Edna's funeral in a nearby Baptist chapel. I was pleased to help her out.

The morning passed pleasantly as he happily played with the toys. Soon it was afternoon. I knew that Les would be helping with the refreshments following the funeral service so I didn't expect her back until late afternoon. Time rolled on and finally she arrived just before 7p.m. The funeral had gone well; she had helped with the refreshments which were back at Edna's home in Manselton.

Les had been praying hard for my situation as I was very heavy on her heart. During the funeral service she felt drawn to the minister of the chapel believing he too had a real faith in the Lord Jesus.

She shared that as she went about her duties helping out during the day, she found herself praying that she would get to speak with the minister. She wasn't even sure what she wanted to say to him. She waited until early evening and reluctantly started getting her coat on to leave. Just then the doorbell rang, and who should be standing there but the minister, Gareth Cheedy.

He explained that on the day of the funeral he never goes back to the family so that they have the space and time to grieve together privately, but in this instance he had felt drawn by God all afternoon to go to Edna's home where the wake was being held.

Les explained that she didn't know what she needed to talk to him about. Wisely, he asked her what was on her heart. She told him of her concern for me and prayer of help that had just been prayed for me. She was amazed as he said part of his ministry was to families with similar issues that my husband had. He suggested I gave him a phone call sometime. She left thanking him for his obedience and hearkening to 'God's prompt'.

Les arrived at my home excited to share what had happened during the day and her meeting with the minister, Gareth Cheedy. After she left, I pondered on all she had shared and decided that I would give him a call later in the evening. He hadn't given a specific day or time to ring. It was at 10p.m. when I had the opportunity to ring. I felt apprehensive and unsure. I was so used to my Anglican tradition.

We were very territorial and each parish was self-contained. Now here I was ringing a minister not in my tradition and outside the parish boundary. Just a few rings and a lady answered - it was his wife Pam saying, 'Hello, is that Sue?' I was astonished because no day or time had been arranged. I hastily said it was and she added that her husband Gareth the minister had left a message in case I'd rung. It was 'If Sue rings, please tell her I've gone to the chapel to pray for her and ask her to ring back at 10.30p.m.' I was amazed and agreed to ring back. My mind was in a whirl. He didn't even know me, yet he'd gone to his chapel to pray for me. I nervously rang at the given time. This time a male voice answered, 'Gareth Cheedy' was his first response. I told him my name. It was as if it had all been planned out by God. He continued that in the chapel God gave him a word for me from Isaiah 43:

Do not be afraid - I will save you. I have called you by name - you are mine. When you pass through deep waters, I will be with you; your troubles will not overwhelm you. When you pass through fire, you will not be burnt; the hard trials that come will not hurt you.

I was speechless! This was the very word that I had been woken up with two years before. This man knew nothing about my life, only that I was in need because of my husband's issues. This was wonderful. The answer to the HELP prayer just 48 hours earlier: how great is His care and love for us!

He arranged a meeting and there began a deep friendship with Gareth, Pam, his wife, and his family that has gone from strength to strength over the years.

You will hear more about this God-given friendship in later chapters. One thing for sure was that the Scripture Gareth gave me was confirmation to me of the time I heard the Lord's voice calling my name and warning me that there would be times ahead that would be extremely challenging, but of God's assurance to me that these times would not overwhelm me. What a promise!

During those months since that phone call, the support I received from Gareth and Pam was indispensable. It enabled me to carry on throughout dark times that often became unbearable. Praying friends around me became like cushions.

I will never forget their help to me. I visited them often over the following few years. We talked, laughed, cried and worshipped God together, and I thoroughly enjoyed Pam's wonderful meals that I shared with them until restrictions were placed on me of whom I could see. I must admit to having 'visits' from them as I served bacon in the cash-and-carry supermarket where I worked part-time. This was the highlight of my week.

I remained in the Anglican Church. I had been christened as a baby and confirmed as a teenager. Les, my friend, had also been through these same traditions of the Anglican Church, which is why I was so shocked when she shared that she was going to be baptised by full immersion.

I felt very uncomfortable with this news and didn't know why. Maybe it was because it defied our tradition. I reluctantly agreed to support her, which I did dutifully. The words that were spoken during the baptismal service were Acts 2:38:

Repent and be baptised, every one of you, in the name of Jesus Christ for the forgiveness of your sins. And you will receive the gift of the Holy Spirit (NIV).

I must admit I was glad when it was over. The words I had heard kept ringing in my ears, *repent and be baptised...repent and be baptised...*over and over again. In fact, the repeating words lasted for two days. Surely God didn't want me to do this? I must be imagining things. But until I gave in and said, 'Yes, I would be baptised,' they didn't go away. I knew I had repented of my sins when I was born again. I also knew that I needed regularly to ask forgiveness for my sins.

Feeling completely out of my comfort zone, I spoke to Gareth and told him what had happened. He agreed to baptise me at my chosen venue, which was in the sea at Langland beach.

I had such a mixed bag of responses: some rejoiced, some called me a heretic. I was reminded of my promise that I would never deny Him anything He asked me to do. I knew this was important and obedience to Him was more important that pleasing friends or a tradition.

As the day approached the butterflies in my stomach got worse as did the weather. We had atrocious weather - thunder and lightning with abundant Welsh-type rain! Gareth rang a few times in the week suggesting we changed the venue for the baptism to his chapel due to this awful weather. I reassured him that we were going to get wet and suggested that those coming to watch bring umbrellas; so it was agreed we would continue as arranged.

The big day arrived and the weather continued to bring heavy downpours, but I was determined to carry on. Lunch was over and I journeyed down to Langland. As we arrived, the dark stormy clouds rolled back to reveal lovely blue skies. The car park was unusually empty for a summer Sunday afternoon and the wet tarmac surface began to steam with the heat of the sun - we wouldn't need umbrellas after all! My nerves left me as we began this special ceremony. My friends gathered around.

On the beach, a guitar strummed as we sang praises to God, with curious dog walkers passing by on the beach hut pathway. I didn't really need confirmation that this way was His will for me but I prayed a strange request. Some might think this is very frivolous and quite irrelevant - asking God for a rainbow. Little did I know how relevant this request was for future times, which I shall share later in the book. It was a wonderful time.

Everyone was gathered close to the edge of the sea as Gareth and I waded through the seaweed. He began to speak out the Scripture passage that had started our journey, Isaiah 43, and he baptised me in the name of Jesus.

Two more friends followed me. Linda decided she too wanted to be baptised, then Doreen with terminal cancer also was drawn by God on the spur of the moment and bravely went confidently into the sea to be baptised. It was a glorious day.

As the evening approached, we continued to sing praises, and in the sky came my answer to prayer - the rainbow I had prayed for. God's promise:

Whenever the rainbow appears in the clouds, I will see it and remember the everlasting covenant between God and all living creatures of every kind on the earth (Genesis 9:16 NIV).

I was truly humbled that the God of the universe would hear my request and because of His great love He would give me this gift. I was overwhelmed with joy. Little did I know that in just three weeks' time my world would fall apart.

7

SHATTERED DREAMS
WITH CHINKS OF LIGHT

The weeks that followed were very busy with the decorating of three rooms in my home. I really enjoyed interior design, although I was just an amateur. I set out to achieve my task. Although very tired, I was content to see my work completed: all the walls sparkling in brilliant white. I loved the satisfaction that it brought.

My husband was on holiday from work. The week had been pretty tense and out of the blue a serious incident occurred that changed my life forever.

I knew I could no longer stay in my marriage. After years of trying to repair the fragile cracks, what seemed to me like an earthquake had taken place. Sadly, it was irreparable, and in the days that followed I prepared for my departure.

The children had to make a very difficult decision which I know to this day they can still remember. My son decided to stay with his father and my daughter decided to come with me. I had put a few personal possessions into the boot of a friend's car.

My daughter and I left heartbroken. Our little Jack Russell dog, Snowy, tried to follow us but as we were now virtually homeless we couldn't take him with us. Babs and her family had told me that if ever I had nowhere to go, I could spend a few nights with them. As I write I am aware that my chest is tightening with remembering this dreaded nightmare. We walked about a mile to Babs' home clutching a bag of owls that I collected and my ten-year-old daughter was carrying her beloved Cindy dolls. The pain was unbearable. I knew my hopes and dreams were over, or so I thought.

I had rung Babs earlier that day and her dear husband Richard and their sons. They opened the doors of their hearts as well as their house. Richard went out shopping to buy all the things we liked to eat. Paul gave up his bedroom for us to sleep 'top and tail'. We were so raw with emotion and this love was cushioning us.

We stayed for the best part of a week. The following week we stayed with friends in a theological college, and finally spent a month with my parents so that my daughter could attend the local school.

Despite the emotions we were both suffering, there was a peace deep within my heart that assured me of the Scripture from Hebrews 12, *I will never leave you or forsake you*. Such a comfort to me. We were classed as homeless and were in the position of being emergency housed by the local council. We were put on the list and we knew it could be months before we were housed.

I have vivid memories of my first ever visit to the Department of Social Security. It was another world to me. Gareth came to support me. As we reached the room, I could see it was filled with people. We could hardly see through the fog of cigarette smoke that had formed. We choked as it burned our throats and noses; even vision was difficult. This was such a negative but necessary experience.

When it was my turn to sit at the open counter that made it possible for all to hear your business, I shared what had happened to me and I needed their help. I was given a pack containing all the forms I would need to take home and fill in. This was daunting, but I took my time and filled them in to the best of my ability.

I heard after some weeks that I was granted the basic amount for Income Support and I would have my child benefit allowance until my daughter finished full-time education.

As friends and my sister's church heard of my plight, I started to have calls offering me household goods and furniture, and white goods for the kitchen. The only thing I had missing was stair carpet. God was supplying all I would need to have a home again.

To everyone's amazement just a month after I had left the matrimonial home, I was offered a flat in an area close to where we had lived.

We viewed the flat - it was a small high-rise flat in a council housing area at a village called Alltwen, near the small town of Pontardawe in the Swansea Valley. The frontage was unkempt, littered with rubbish, broken concrete, long grass and broken glass strewed throughout it. It was in need of cleaning and redecorating. However, this didn't faze me.

The views were amazing. I could see miles down the valley to the sea at Swansea in the distance, so I accepted the flat knowing we would be safe there, and that it was near to a school for my daughter. I knew God had provided this place of safety for me and that whatever difficulties I may encounter, He would be in it with me: what a comfort!

I began making plans for the move. I had only my personal belongings and an antique sewing machine table that I had made into a desk. My nana had made our clothes on this machine when we were children. I treasured it. These were put into the carport for me to collect. I was very keen not to take furniture and household goods from the matrimonial home as my son was still living there and his sister would be visiting her brother and father regularly. I wanted the home to remain welcoming for them all.

Friends and I tackled cleaning the flat and soon it started to take shape. Gill came to help, carrying a box that was packed with items that we would need, from cleaning materials to soaps for the bathroom, and a brightly-coloured cheerful orange towel. I was so blessed.

The worst part must have been the downstairs storeroom. It was filled to the brim with black bags bulging with soiled nappies. It was a very unpleasant experience, and a great relief when the council came to take them away. I hastily disinfected every part of the storeroom which in time became a place for my moped to be housed.

Dear Mum persuaded Dad that they needed a new sideboard, dining table and chairs. I knew she had only done that so that I could have hers. As she waited for hers to be delivered, she brought the patio table, chairs and umbrella in from their garden, and set them up as their eating area until her new dining room suite was delivered. She was quite a woman was my lovely mum!

Dad heard that his next-door neighbour was throwing out her large lounge carpet. He asked if I could have it rather than throwing it away. She agreed, so we carried it onto his lawn and proceeded to cut it to the measured shape of the lounge in the flat. It was a great start even though it was going to be a bit like a jigsaw puzzle patched with so many bits. But I was so grateful.

I had made a list of all the household goods so generously offered to me. Gareth kindly offered to hire a van. He contacted all those who were contributing and arranged to go from house-to-house to collect.

If anyone has lost their home and possessions you will know how vulnerable you feel - it's very scary. The future was uncertain. But knowing Who was holding the future gave me a peace that passes understanding.

The moving day arrived. Gareth set off on his mission. We arrived at the flat and awaited the van to arrive with furniture and household items. This was very different from the first house we had worked hard for, as we furnished it with new items. I forced back the emotions of the circumstances that had brought me to this place just over a month previously and stayed focused on the task in hand.

Just before lunchtime the van arrived, full to the brim with furniture, and all I would need to start again. We had a flight of steps for the men to manoeuvre. The dining furniture was one of the first items to arrive. Family and close friends had arrived to help.

I fondly remember Mum scurrying to her basket of goodies. Out came the tablecloth that she draped over the table, and laid it full of delicious delights made by herself and Pam, Gareth's wife. What a feast that first meal was! We all worked tirelessly, with the result that by early evening we had curtains hung and furniture in its place.

My daughter's bedroom was ready for her, and white goods fitted all ready for use in the kitchen. We even had pictures on the walls. More amazing, everything was matching! God is so clever.

We kept unpacking numerous boxes full of items that I would need. It was so humbling, the generosity of people; some didn't even know me but had heard of my plight. Mum decided to pray for more saucepans. To her astonishment, within days and without asking anyone, they started arriving in abundance. We hastily retracted that prayer…how amazing is that?

By the evening we were pretty exhausted but overwhelmed with the love I had received. We said our deepest gratitude to everyone as they left for a well-needed rest and sleep.

My daughter was tucked up in her new room and I settled into my bedroom with a fold-up z-bed that would be my temporary one until I could afford to buy a single bed. In the corner of the room I put my special desk that was made from my nana's treadle machine with my personal treasures that I had managed to bring with me.

I reflected over the day. God had been with me every step of the way, even to the way of keeping my dignity. We didn't look like homeless people with nothing. The way He had orchestrated the arrival of the van made it look like I was the same as anyone else moving from one place to another, my dignity intact.

The verse from Isaiah 43 He had given had said that I was precious in His sight. He had shown me such love and provision that day. I felt the tangible love of God as Abba Father to me - His child, precious in His sight! I fell soundly asleep that night with praise on my lips knowing I was safe and secure in His arms. To describe how I was feeling is very difficult - there were so many mixed emotions.

A sense of safety and freedom ran through them like a gold thread, but the grief and sadness of a marriage ending caused me much pain.

We saw God's hand in so many ways. The concrete jungle that we looked out on from our window was a subject of prayer for Babs. She knew I loved my garden and had lost it along with my home. Just weeks after she had prayed, along came a bulldozer digging up the old concrete and rubble. The area was beautifully landscaped with grass and trees: a wonderful outlook.

I could see that God was using this time to refine me and knock off rough edges. I had left a new private housing estate; we had watched the house being built brick by brick. The houses were all well-kept, gardens trim and laden with seasonal flowers. Everyone had jobs and were living their dreams, or so it seemed on the outside.

What a contrast! My circumstances of being emergency-housed had propelled me into a council estate living amongst unemployed people, on the dole since leaving school with no incentive to change, single parents with social issues. For many, hope had gone out of the window.

It was a culture shock for me as I had entered their world. I loved this new-found freedom. I would suddenly decide to bake a cake at 10p.m. or put on my make-up, just to take it off again. I had felt like a prisoner for so long.

During the first week of school, I decided to explore the area. Just across the road, behind a dilapidated play area, were trees. I followed the path which led to a small wooded area. I could hear the sound of water. As I went further down, I could see the River Tawe glistening in the sunshine, the water rippling over the pebbles. I was amazed at the beauty and it was just minutes from where I had been given a place to live.

For those first two weeks straight after my daughter left for school, I would give the flat a quick tidy up, pack a picnic lunch and flask of coffee, pack my rucksack with my Walkman, praise music, writing pad and pen, my Bible and a book. With my folding chair slung over my shoulder off I'd go for the rest of the day to this little oasis just a stone's throw from where I lived, returning home before the end of the school day. I cannot tell you how healing this time was - it was like being on holiday without costing anything!

Those traumatic weeks that had led up to me leaving my husband had taken its toll on me. My security had been shaken and my future unknown. Those two weeks sitting in the sunshine in the beauty of this peaceful place beside the river gave me time to reflect, talk with God and receive the balm of healing to start this next part of my journey with Him. I would often return to this oasis and amazingly when I moved on to my next home the whole area was demolished for a new bypass road system to be built that ran beside the River Tawe.

8

NEW BEGINNINGS

My daughter took many months to settle. She missed her dad terribly as well as her brother, although after some time he started to be a regular visitor to us. The adjustment took its toll. The decision to leave my husband was the most difficult I had ever had to make.

I knew it would have long-lasting effects on the children. But I believe to this day that despite the pain they suffered it would have been so much worse if I had stayed in the unhappiness that we were all experiencing.

I had begun to receive my Income Support. This was a new thing for me which I found quite scary. I had not had the purse strings when I lived with my husband, so handling and managing a tight budget was going to be a challenge for me. I reminded myself of that wonderful truth that God was my provider.

Our first shop in the local supermarket was difficult as I didn't know how much money I had to spend on food. My utility bills were an unknown quantity to me, so I was being extra careful. We always used a butter-type product but I wasn't sure if we could now afford it - even margarine seemed expensive.

I arrived back at the flat feeling quite deflated and tried to resist the dark cloud that wanted to engulf me. One hour later there was a knock at my door. There stood Babs panting after she had climbed the stairs to reach me. She said she had been at home praying when God had said to take me a pound of butter! Bless her heart, she immediately went to the shop, bought it and brought it to me. We laughed and laughed as she said they couldn't even afford to buy butter for themselves. Another occasion a similar thing happened when Babs arrived with a large packet of toilet rolls after hearing God asking her to deliver them to me.

One particular day I had walked to the supermarket in Pontardawe and just before I got there it was as if my eyes were taken to focus on the daises, called ox-eye daisy *Leucanthemum vulgare* in this instance, growing freely at the side of the road. I sensed God say to me, 'This is your garden.' So each week I would pick a bunch and take them home, place them in a vase and they'd last all week until I went shopping again. I understood the saying 'fresh as a daisy' because they would look cheerful and lovely all week. It was as if my Heavenly Father was giving me a bouquet of flowers: I loved them! It spoke to me of God's loving care for me even at this level.

He knew what I needed - I would never have thought that a God who created the world would care about such mundane requirements that we have, yet He does. In Matthew 6:26, Jesus says:

Look at the birds of the air; they do not sow or reap or store away in barns, and yet your Heavenly Father feeds them. Are you not much more valuable than they? (NIV)

It speaks of a loving Father who cares about everything that concerns me and for all those who put their trust in Him.

Just days after I moved in, God started to send me ladies who needed TLC and a listening ear, perhaps to pray with or give some advice to. I found this such a privilege to be so trusted. They would often sit beside my little converted sewing machine table and pour out the contents of their hearts to me. It was wonderful the way God would bring them comfort and hope.

Just weeks after we moved in God brought twelve-year-old Cath into our lives. I had a call from an old curate friend who asked me if I would visit her. Cath's mum had been diagnosed with multiple sclerosis when Cath was three years old.

On Boxing Day when Cath was nine years old sadly her mum died, but knowing she had come to faith in Jesus was a great comfort to Cath in years to come. Cath moved in with her paternal grandparents until they split up, and was then abruptly shipped off to her maternal grandparents at a village near the flat I had moved to. This had been a very hard young life.

She was a little older than my daughter. When we first met her she was distant and withdrawn, obviously very sad and displaced as she began adapting to her new surroundings; but she was loved and well cared for by her maternal grandparents. I remember her grandfather saying, 'You can and you will'! They brought such love and stability into Cath's life.

In just a few months she began to open up to me and very soon we became the best of friends. I loved her dearly, she became a member of our family, and still is. Her faith even as a young child had kept her strong throughout her turbulent times.

She grew to be a wonderful young lady and remains strong in the Lord and a wonderful role model as a wife and mother.

After some weeks, I had heard that there was a lady called Jean who lived just across the road from our flats. She was quite a character - streetwise and well-known to the small community. Her life had been very difficult, but she had fought through and survived.

I heard she had had an encounter with God and was told that I had moved into the flats. She sought me out and started visiting 'Shalom'. She would bring her younger children in with her - two lovely girls. As they came through the door, she would say to them, 'Sit down, we are on holy ground.' She would ask me to pray for her. 'Ask Jesus for my zigzag,' she would say. Her faith was simple - it was her way to ask for the Holy Spirit to fill her. The physical experience when it happened felt like a zigzag going through her body, hence the expression!

Jean shared with me all about her life. She was a very brave lady. I admired her so much and thanked God for bringing her into my life.

Her schooling was lacking as she was kept home and therefore couldn't read or write. She asked me to teach her but she wanted to learn by reading the Bible. I remember one day Jean had gone on a Sunday school trip with her children to Tenby. The done thing those days was to buy presents to bring home. I was given a Christian card. Jean had no idea what it said on it because she hadn't yet mastered reading, but was thrilled to know that it was the exact word that God had been speaking to me about, Matthew 5:14-16 (NIV):

You are the light of the world. A town built on a hill cannot be hidden. Neither do people light a lamp and put it under a bowl. Instead they put it on its stand, and it gives light to everyone in the house. In the same way, let your light shine before others, that they may see your good deeds and glorify your Father in heaven.

I marvelled at the way the Lord had used Jean to confirm this word to me. We rejoiced together and thanked God for His wondrous ways. As Christmas was just weeks away, I remember her coming to my door with two carrier bags full of exotic foods. She had taken all the best things from her hamper that she had been saving for since summer and had brought them to me. What a sacrifice!

As winter came upon us we would snuggle up each evening in sleeping bags with hot water bottles keeping our toes toasty. We conserved as much heat as we could to save on cost. There was little money as I didn't work. In those days you stayed at home to look after the children until they were able to stay on their own during work hours.

My clothes came out of black bags of discarded clothes from friends who had a child of similar age to my daughter and ones that would fit me. He knew I loved M&S clothes and most times to my delight I would find the bag contained clothes from that store and just what I needed to have.

Jumble sales were very popular in those days. Car boot sales were unheard of. Very often we would scan through items, especially bric-a-brac, and pick up some bargains to make the house more cosy. I set about decorating almost straight away.

It was the first time my daughter was going for the day with her father. After she left the flat, it was very silent and I felt very alone. I knew I had painting to do in the hallway but self-pity began to set in and started to sap my energy. There was a big cupboard in the hallway and I remember thinking why should I paint the inside of the cupboard when nobody would see it. I immediately felt reprimanded by God who said I was to paint the inside of the cupboard because He lived here too! Reluctantly I emptied the cupboard and started to give it a lick of white paint. Something quite amazing happened. Immediately the awful dark feeling of self-pity left me and was replaced with peace and thankfulness. His Grace is always sufficient and an awesome gift for us.

We settled in slowly to this new way of life. There was lots of sadness but it was mingled with joy too as the weight of the tensions and stress I'd suffered for many years had now gone.

Our first holiday since moving to the flat was an Easter Christian conference called Spring Harvest. It was held in the Butlins Holiday Camp at Minehead. Gareth and Pam organised it and a few families were going together.

I was still feeling pretty vulnerable and when I arrived I was aware of being surrounded by happy couples, and my singleness felt exposed and painful. I was strangely drawn to their wedding rings and diamond engagement rings. They belonged to each other. I was on my own now.

It's true you can be lonely even in a room full of your favourite friends. I went to many seminars and worship nights. We took it in turns to babysit the children. On the Wednesday evening it was the girls' time to go out while the men babysat. Halfway through the worship was stopped and a word was given that she felt that God had put it on her heart to sing this chorus. We stood to sing these words:

Lord, You are more precious than silver;
Lord, You are more costly than gold;
Lord, You are more beautiful than diamonds;
And nothing I desire compares with You.

As we sang these words, I knew they were for me. I understood why I had been drawn to the couples, their wedding and engagement rings. The heartache lifted and I knew that these words were to be my love song to Jesus.

Laughter rang in our chalets for the rest of the week and we all went home feeling different and grateful for the wonderful company of each other and the gift of releasing laughter.

***

When I think of the many modes of communication we have now, it seems archaic to have to run to the phone box to make a call as I did during those eighteen months in the flat.

We named the flat 'Shalom'. Hebrew words go beyond their spoken pronunciation. Each Hebrew word conveys feeling, intent and emotion. 'Shalom' is more than just simply peace: it is a complete peace. It is a feeling of contentment, completeness, wholeness, well-being and harmony. It was indeed this to me.

The flat might have been filled with everyone else's bits of furniture, but it was filled with love. The name was so apt after the years of disharmony I had experienced. You will see as you journey with me through the years that the other homes God led me to also bore the name 'Shalom' because He was and is with me every step of the way.

There were many challenges during this time, which were painful. One was the divorce. My husband divorced me as I had left the matrimonial home and he had found it impossible to live with me anymore because God had become number one in my life.

I had grounds to divorce him that would have been a biblical reason, but I didn't feel God wanted me to do this. As I said in an earlier chapter, I have chosen to keep his dignity and not go into these details. Some friends were praying for reconciliation between us. I knew it had reached the point of no return. There was no indication from God that He had a plan to restore this relationship. It was as if He had raised His hand in authority saying, 'Enough.'

I was pleased he quickly met a new lady. She was a good woman: l liked her. Eve was a hard worker and it was a good match. He needed her strength and a determined spirit to support him. She was kind to my children and was an excellent mother to her own two boys. They soon married and began a new life together.

Each day I would sing praises to a God who loved me and had rescued me from despair. However, I found that I was beginning to miss certain aspects of my last home. Silly things really, but they began to become an issue. One thing was my own washing line. In the flat we were allocated half a line each. All the lines were positioned together at the side of the building. Some people left their washing out for days. The lines often needed regular cleaning as the cords would put dirty marks on the washing.

The other thing I had begun to miss was my garden. Gardening had become therapeutic to me and a way of escape. I loved the grafting of hard work and the contentment at the end of the task to see areas turned into something beautiful. I found myself repenting of this because I thought how ungrateful I was becoming. Sometime later I could see that this was actually God shoe-horning me out of my comfort zone.

I met Ann and her young sons. She had visited me at my flat for some advice. She invited me to her home in Trebanos. It was a cosy two-bedroomed house with a large garden. Ann was also a single mum and had lived in dire circumstances which had forced her to leave. She had since met someone else and was contemplating the next step in her life. She mentioned that she had considered moving and asked me how I would feel about a transfer. Ann would move into the flat and I would have her house if the council agreed. My comfort zone was shattered! I had got used to my surroundings of eighteen months. I was settled and managing to budget the cost of running the flat. My daughter had finally settled and we had even managed to get used to the fact that a working prostitute with a missing window lived next door.

What if the outgoings would be higher than that of the flat? All these things were whizzing through my mind.

Ann encouraged me to look at the advantages of moving to her house. The garden with a view would be such a bonus for us…and our own washing line! Ann also had a phone connected. Up until then to make a call I had to go to the nearest phone box. Making calls was always difficult because I wouldn't and couldn't leave my daughter on her own; also she wouldn't need to change schools.

The spanner in the works was when Ann revealed to me that she would use my flat only as storage. Straightaway I knew I could not agree to this exchange.

This flat had been a place of refuge for me to be emergency-housed. It needed to be available for another homeless person, not just to store furniture in. And perhaps as important, it was not being honest with the council who were her landlords.

Ann understood my point but categorically pointed out that there was no way I would be allowed to have tenancy of her house unless I did it her way.

Overnight how I battled with this! I had set my heart on her house. It seemed to make sense. I was doing a little cleaning job for an invalid friend who lived just a few hundred yards from the house. Deep down I knew it was wrong and decided to stick to my guns and trust God that if this was the house for me, then it would come into being. Ann honoured my decision.

I contacted the council just before Ann gave notice of tenancy. They interviewed me and said I had a good case but could not make any firm decision. It was nail-biting time. But I trusted Him for the outcome: I only wanted His provision. Weeks went by. The weather was bitterly cold, and many homes had frozen pipes and floods so any empty houses were being given to those who had had to move out.

Providentially, the house in Trebanos also had frozen pipes; they hadn't burst but they couldn't put new tenants there. Early February I had that long-awaited call to say they had assigned the Trebanos house to me: I danced to the Lord with great joy that day!

We left the flat with gratefulness for the safety and refuge it had become to us, hoping that it would also be a place of *shalom* for the next people who would become tenants there.

We crossed the River Tawe with our belongings and made our way just a mile-and-a-half to our new home. I knew straightaway that this was the right move. My parents were with me helping me unpack, and because Ann had left some carpets, it made life a lot easier. By the time my daughter had arrived from school, we had most things in place. It looked lovely.

That evening in the quietness of our own company, I looked out of the window at the long private garden with so much potential - a garden I could make into something beautiful - space to enjoy creation, sunbathe even, and oh! the joy to have a washing line to myself. Things like this we take for granted until they are taken away from us.

The house was on a long, quiet road. We were the first semi-detached council house, with private housing to the right and opposite us. It felt so safe to be there.

This was our Shalom*2*. The view was wonderful as we looked out onto a mountain in the distance - I believe it's called the Drummau mountain.

The house comprised a compact kitchen, with just outside two outbuildings attached to the house. In time these became a very handy utility room and a tool shed with a workbench. There was a cosy lounge and a front room which had now become our dining room. Upstairs there were two decent-sized bedrooms and a bathroom. We had gas central heating.

Spring would soon be on its way followed by summer and sunbathing times in our very own garden. As I went to bed that night, I could never have guessed what God had in store for me in the coming seasons!

We quickly adjusted to our new abode and loved it. Trebanos has its own post office and shop, with a couple of pubs and hairdressers, so it was quite a handy place to live.

The added joy for me was to discover that just across the main road from my new home led to a canal path which was a wonderful walk along the side of the canal with all its greenery: either to Clydach one way through a beautiful park or to Pontardawe the other way. What a bonus!

Not long after we moved in, friends from Cardiff needed to rehouse their beloved Yorkshire terrier called Bonnie. I didn't need much persuasion as I was very partial to this breed as my parents had a Yorkie called Kim that we adored. We jumped at the chance and Bonnie became part of our family. She adored the walks along the canal with lots of trees and greenery to sniff at.

GOD IN THE TRAGEDY

Mike's story

News came to me about the Davies family; I was so fond of them and had been praying for them for some years. They had gone on a boating holiday and had a wonderful time together, and then the worst tragedy struck. Their beloved son and newly-married son-in-law had gone overboard and drowned. I was devastated and became so angry with God. How could a loving God have allowed this to happen?

I had been praying for years that they would come to know Jesus as their personal Saviour, and now this had happened. I was beside myself and knew I had to vent my feelings. I was due to start redecorating the kitchen, so I stripped every bit of paper from the kitchen walls with tears and sorrow for this beautiful family who had lost their son and new son-in-law.

A few days later my daughter and I went to visit them. It was a cold evening and I was trembling at the thought of what I would say to them. I thought they would be so angry with God, and I as a committed Christian might well take the full brunt of it.

I gingerly knocked on their door. A light went on in their hallway; I was holding my breath. Mike answered the door. I was trying to get the words out about my deepest sympathy and how sorry I was. He gently beckoned us into their home. He didn't look angry at all but there was a serenity and sense of deep peace in the home and around him. He took us into his lounge, sat us down and proceeded to tell us the tale: how they had had such a wonderful holiday together with the newly-weds. They were taking the boat back to the boatyard at the end of their holiday. Their son accidentally fell into the water and the son-in-law jumped in to help him. But within minutes they disappeared out of sight and both drowned.

A community of Anglican nuns had taken them in overnight and tended to them, feeding them, warming them and giving them God's love: this helped them all to begin their journey seeking God in this situation, and eventually led to them giving themselves to Jesus, and He became their personal Saviour. I had no words, but a hug of deep compassion assured him that I would be there for him and his family.

We walked back in absolute awe of what God had done. I was deeply repenting for venting my anger at Him. Does God make mistakes? Never! He turned this tragedy into a life change - eternal life for that family. This would not make them escape the deep sadness and grief they were to experience for many, many years. But He had made His home in their lives so He could bear the sorrows with them and cushion and love them through their pain.

THE GIFT OF RON

My life had been centred around making a happy and stable life for my daughter and me. She saw her dad regularly, and occasionally stayed overnight with them all. My son was still with his father and visited often to see us. He was then working in the area which was a real bonus.

My social life consisted of church activities mostly, and I kept in touch with friends as and when I could. I would use my moped to get from place to place locally, with a few hairy moments encountering fallen autumn leaves and icy roads that would make biking hazardous: grazed knees and hurt pride were often the scene of the day.

Some friends had gone to a Christian conference in beautiful Cumbria on the Scottish Borders and had met a gentleman named Ron from Leeds.

Let me tell you a little about him. Ron was divorced, though not out of choice. He had also become homeless for some weeks before friends took him in. He was impressed by a work colleague called Tim. Tim was a committed Christian and each lunchtime would sit with his lunch reading his Bible. Ron talked with him about his faith as Ron was definitely on a spiritual journey, looking into many other faiths and was interested in spiritualism and séances. Tim and his wife Jenny befriended Ron and his interest in Christianity started to grow. They invited Ron to a house-group to learn more about each other and Jesus. Very soon Ron made a decision for Jesus and after some months of nurturing, destroyed all his books on other gods, religions and New Age teachings.

The fascination with mediums and séances had been with him a long time. He could stop the hands of his grandmother's wall clock just by looking at it. He was told by the medium that he had that gift, a gift of healing from God. He believed them. One day about six months after he became a born-again Christian, he had gone to a meeting of one of the mediums. He was wearing a small lapel cross in his jacket. In the silence, she was having great difficulty connecting with the spirit world.

She looked up, then looked over to Ron and said, 'Remove that cross, young man.' He knew from that moment on that this was wrong. It was not of the God he had come to know and love, but of the enemy Satan. He never went back there again. That gives you a bit of a background.

My friends loved meeting him with his heart for singles, and passion for homeless people. He loved sharing the Lord with those he met. They told me about him and suggested I contacted him as he had similar interests. They knew that I hadn't got any interest in a relationship as I was quite happy for it to be just my daughter and me.

A few months after the conference in Cumbria, Ron happened to ring Lesley when I was visiting her. She mentioned I had called in to visit her and asked if he would like to say hello to me. He seemed a kind man and we decided to write as pen-pals to encourage each other in our faith. We did this for some months.

We happened to be on holiday in Bradford. The friends we were staying with asked if there was anything I would like to do. I suggested maybe visiting my pen pal in nearby Leeds. We arranged a meeting and met him at his flat with his two children, Mark and Gareth. I thought what a good man; he seemed like a modern 'friar tuck'. Ron and the boys came to Bradford to visit before we left to come home to Swansea.

The weekend I came home there was the Summer Apostolic Convention. I was invited to go to an epilogue late on the Friday evening and decided to go. Lilian was picking me up. It was good to go although I can't remember anything at all about the meeting so many years ago, but I can vividly remember what happened after it!

The epilogue meeting always finished late. By the time we were getting into the car, there was a slight chill in the evening air. As we journeyed back to Swansea, I became aware of heat radiating from my breastbone, around my lower ribs to the rib cage in my back. I checked the back of the seat which remained cool. The rest of my body remained cool.

By the next day I felt God showing me that He had given me a 'new heart'. Of course, I still had the heart I was born with, but He had done something very significant with the old damaged one that had suffered much heartache. It's a mystery to me how He does these things, but all I can say is He does. Amazingly, the heat that I had felt the night before was exactly the area where a person would be cut for heart surgery. The purpose for this 'heart surgery' had yet to be revealed, but I didn't have to wait long to wait to find out.

That weekend I reflected on my meeting with Ron and his sons. Ron had been quite tired and was recovering from a chest infection. He loved having his sons at the weekend and he was also very active in his Anglican church at Burley. Another passion was helping the homeless on the streets of Leeds. Currently unemployed through no fault of his own, he was often seen in a café in the city sitting with a homeless person who would be enjoying a steaming mug of tea and sandwiches. He would also take flasks of tea out with him to town and share them with anyone who needed to talk and have a hot cuppa.

He loved telling people about Jesus. He never forgot that for a short time he too had been homeless and knew how it felt to have an extended arm of kindness reaching for him.

I sensed he really needed a break with the boys. Money was tight for him but I had a little spare cash available for bus fares for them and invited them to my home for a week's holiday.

My daughter was going to be away with her father and his new family. I knew I could offer Ron and his boys my home.

I would spend the day with them and then stay at Lilian's home which was a couple of miles away. I put this suggestion to him. He was very thankful, but would first pray about it to see if this was God's will for them. I liked his total trust in God, not doing his own thing.

A day or so later he got back to me and said he would love to take up the invitation. He had asked someone in Leeds to also pray about this invitation. They came back to him saying, 'Is there a mountain nearby where Sue lives?' When I told him the house looked out onto a mountain, that was his confirmation and he told me he would be delighted to accept my invitation as it was school holidays.

The following week Ron and his boys travelled from Leeds to Swansea on the coach. A long journey, but they were excited to be having a holiday near the sea. My local Christian friends arranged outings and ferried us around the Gower coast and various venues that they thoroughly enjoyed.

It was lovely having them and seeing them enjoying themselves so much. Ron and I got on so well; we had much in common, especially about commitment to Jesus.

The end of the week came very quickly. It was the Friday morning. I had arrived as arranged to make them their breakfast. The boys were taken to some activity that they wanted to do, leaving Ron and me to relax and chat until they returned. I was in the kitchen when I clearly heard God speak to me. He said, 'Ask Ron what he is thinking.' I promptly went into the dining room where Ron was sitting at the table. We were on the same wavelength so it wasn't strange for him to know that God can speak this way. When I told him what I believed God had told me to say, he gulped and nearly fell off the chair! This was quite a reaction I thought, but I reassured him and said, 'Just say what you were thinking.'

I could see he was plucking up courage and finally he spoke it out: 'Well, I was just thinking how I would like to spend the rest of my life with you!' What shocked me most was my reply. Unrehearsed, unplanned, totally out of character for me who never did anything in a hurry, I opened my mouth to speak and out came, 'So would I!' I don't know who was in more shock - Ron or me! This certainly was not on my agenda. We looked at each other, disbelieving what we had said to each other, and gave each other a platonic hug.

It dawned on me the significance of the experience the week before when I believed God had given me a new heart, figuratively speaking. The old heart could not have had the capacity to love again. But the new heart, the heart of flesh that God had given me, was capable of being able to love and receive love again.

Their summer holiday had come to an end and they had to return to Leeds. We had no idea when they arrived that God had plans for our lives to be joined together. Ron did confess some months later that his late grandmother was Welsh, and he had been praying for a Welsh wife. It was a good job I didn't know at the time, or I would have run a mile with the old heart I then had.

The only means of communication for us in the 1980s was good old letter writing and the corded telephone. I'm glad I cannot remember just how much our bills were for stamps and phone calls - suffice to know they were high, very high!

When I think back, I didn't really appreciate the impact our new relationship would have on my daughter and of course my family and friends. The best way to describe our growing relationship is an old-fashioned word but totally apt for us: it is 'courtship', which means a period during which a couple develops a romantic relationship before getting married. We weren't drawn together by sexual chemistry. It was an arranged marriage - not arranged by any human intervention, but by God. This was His plan for us.

I remember one evening some weeks after Ron had returned to Leeds, I was looking at engagement rings in the Argos catalogue. I felt a bit guilty at the time thinking was I being materialistic. I didn't mention it to Ron but out of the blue on one of our regular phone chats he said he had been thinking about an engagement ring and if he sold the television and video player then he would have enough money to buy one. I answered very decisively that he should not sell the television and video. He used them to watch programmes and films when the boys came to stay each weekend, and I hastily added that if God wanted us to have an engagement ring then He would provide. We sealed that request in prayer and carried on our late evening talk together.

Early the next morning my dear friend Babs arrived. She knew nothing of my conversation with Ron the evening before. She asked me if we had been praying about anything specific. I told her about the engagement ring conversation, but before I could complete it she shook her head in amazement and said that God had told her to offer me one of her heirloom antique rings. We were so excited! She promptly got up and asked me to come home with her and pick one of the rings.

Soon we were in her kitchen at the familiar kitchen table that we sat at for hours over the years as I picked a beautiful gold ring encrusted with diamonds and sapphires. What astounded us is that it fitted. Babs suggested we checked with Ron that he wouldn't be offended at her most generous gift. Needless to say, he was more than delighted and thankful to God. We decided that on his next visit in a month's time in September we would get engaged.

The little gang of friends, who had been so kind in making Ron's holiday in August with the boys such a huge success, decided they wanted to arrange the engagement party for us. Such kindness! Our conversations from Swansea to Leeds were always heart-warming as our relationship grew, and over the weeks we made the decision that Ron would leave Leeds and live in Trebanos when we eventually married.

Ron arrived in the September. We planned for him to sleep at Babs' and Richard's home not too far away. What may sound really weird in this day and age is that to this point we hadn't even kissed one another! We were like 'babes in the wood'.

He loved the engagement ring that was such a generous gift from Babs. The morning of our engagement party God gave us a special gift. He put a huge rainbow in the sky for us. He knew how important rainbows were to me. I felt that this again was a confirmation of bringing us together. The party was a huge success and we got that same little group praying for the date that we should get married!

All this was very exciting, and somewhat scary as we prepared to mould our families together.

Catherine would visit regularly. She had an old head on her shoulders and being my daughter's peer, she would comfort and help her, as she was coming to terms with the forthcoming wedding and having a stepdad. We underestimate how hard it is for stepchildren, especially as new love can be all-consuming.

Our difficulties with one of Ron's sons presented itself after our marriage. The other difficulty we encountered was from some of our Christian friends. We were both divorced, and remarriage at the time was shunned by the traditional Anglican Church. Some even doubted that God had brought us together. We both knew that our previous marriages sadly breaking up would not have been our choice. We were grieved as we saw some friends step back from us as we pressed forward into what we believed was God's will for our lives together.

One book that really helped was *God is a Matchmaker* by Derek Prince. This was enlightening, and a challenge for us at the first instance. Then we shared it with others and by the time our marriage date approached, we felt we had their blessing too, which was everything to us. Soon after our engagement, our praying friends gave us the date for the wedding - March,11th, 1988.

When Ron returned to Leeds, he began making plans for the move. We had talked about which of our homes to settle in and decided he would move to Pontardawe at Christmas time and would rent a small room above a local pub until the time we got married in March.

Christmas was here and Ron arrived with his personal belongings and books. I have never seen so many books; we knew we would have to build a mini library by shelving lots of walls in the house. Before he left Leeds, he freely gave his furniture away to those in need.

Every morning Ron would walk from his digs at Pontardawe and arrive with his infamous carrier bag in time for breakfast, then leave again after supper for his mile walk to his temporary home until our March wedding.

Time was drawing near to the big day. We had decided to get married in a registry office as we had come out of the Anglican Church at that stage. It was a hard decision because it was the only tradition I knew. But I also knew that I couldn't go along with some of the stands that were being made. Sadly, I felt I had to leave. We knew that the most important part for us was making our vows to one another and to the Lord. We decided we would do this a day or so before the wedding on our beloved canal walk.

About eight weeks before the wedding Ron reminded me that we needed to go to County Hall to book and to choose our wedding rings. We gathered our weekly money together: combined it totalled £55, although this was usually used for food and utilities. The Lord had showed me in Scripture, Ecclesiastes 4:12: *A cord of three strands is not quickly broken.* I thought how wonderful if I could find a wedding ring with three different golds entwined together like a triangle - Jesus as the head in our marriage, with Ron and me joined with Him.

We set off for Swansea with all the money we had to last the week. We gave notice to the Registry Office. Then we started our search for a wedding ring. I couldn't believe it because in the window of the first jeweller's shop we looked at was the exact ring I wanted and the only one in the shop like it. Three strands of different gold were intertwined to make it the perfect choice. The other amazing thing, it was on sale at half price! Originally, we were only going to put a deposit on the rings but this had to be bought outright. We came out of the shop absolutely delighted.

The next was to get Ron a ring. All his life he had given to others and put his own needs in second place. Even then he said he would have his ring from Woolworths and get one later in the year. I insisted that he too would have a shiny real gold ring for our wedding day. We went to the second jeweller's and there was a sale on. Ron picked the ring he liked; this too was half price. He asked if we could put a deposit on it, but I spoke up and said we would pay in full that day.

The last bit of shopping was a spray of powder-blue flowers that I would put on my bag on the day. Then it was home. We had our return tickets and just a pound or two left from the money we had used to last the week. We were too pleased with our purchases to worry about how we would manage for the rest of the week. Ron left for his digs that evening very pleased with our lovely bargains.

He arrived for breakfast the next morning. Soon after, there was a knock on the door. It was a friend on his way to work. He seemed embarrassed and completely out of his comfort zone. He hurriedly explained that God had told him to give us the contents of the envelope he thrust into our hands. He was totally miffed and said nothing like this had ever happened to him before, and we were never to say who he was.

Within seconds he had scurried to his car and was gone. We closed the door and opened the envelope. To our amazement it contained three times the amount we had spent the day before! We had more than enough for our food, gas and electricity, with enough left over to buy Ron not one, but two pairs of shoes. We could hardly contain our joy. We felt God had honoured us as we obeyed what He had asked of us. What an awesome Father God who cares for all our needs.

The wedding plans continued. We had a tight budget. The reception was being held in my little home and all the food was being done by friends who had offered to spend the day looking after us and serving all the culinary delights.

The big day arrived and we set off for the ceremony at County Hall with friends and family. When we returned home the friends who had worked so hard had dressed in black waitress clothes looking professional and did an amazing job for us. The atmosphere of celebration and love made it a day to remember.

Our honeymoon was a gift for us. A beautiful cottage holiday on the Gower Peninsula, with open fires and lovely walks. We even had some early spring sunshine. We were so grateful. We looked forward to our return to at last start a life together and a ministry to serve the Lord in all He had planned for us.

My daughter had been looked after by my aunt at our home. When we arrived, there was quite a surprise in store for us. My son had had a big fall-out with his dad and had moved in with us! The two-bedroomed house needed to stretch to an extra bed space. We bought a sofa bed and he occupied the dining room during the night times. He lived with us for several months, which was so good for him to bond with Ron, his new stepdad. As the summer months approached, he set up home with his girlfriend as they waited for the arrival of my grandchild.

Back in Leeds we were aware that Ron's eldest son, Mark, who was nearly fourteen at the time, was grieving. He missed his dad so much. The distance between the two cities meant it was not possible for him to visit very often. During the summer holidays Mark came and stayed. I remember with horror the first time we had gone to the seaside with him. Mark had gone into the sea. The weather had brought out the crowds and we quickly lost sight of him. Frantically we scanned the sea line, but there was no sign of him. It felt like hours as we searched for him. In my mind I was rehearsing my speech to his mother back in Leeds, how we had lost him forever to the sea. My stomach was churning. We were just about to raise the alarm when we saw a figure that looked like him in the distance coming out of the sea: we dared to hope that it was him. What a relief we felt. He was oblivious to all the drama. Mark was unaware that the current had carried him so far away. We breathed out again, so thankful to God for keeping him safe.

Mark returned home and was even more unsettled. As the autumn approached, we all made the decision together that the best thing for Mark's welfare was that he came to live with us permanently. We can never underestimate the effect of blending two families together - it is one of the most difficult tasks ever. It takes courage, oodles of divine patience and time for it to happen. It can take years. If I hadn't believed that

God had the Master plan for our new lives together, then many times I would have thought this was an impossible situation. But we survived - just!

As summer approached, just a few months after our wedding we were doing a big decorating job for the disabled lady I helped with household chores. It was very hot and the work was strenuous. Ron started to develop flu-type symptoms but insisted on carrying on to finish the task in hand. He finished the work and they thanked him for his generosity of giving his time to help them.

The symptoms continued from days to weeks and into months. He was given different medication but nothing made any difference. His energy levels were depleted and he found life very hard. Because of this he couldn't get work.

After eighteen months he was diagnosed with a condition called myalgic encephalomyelitis (ME) or chronic fatigue syndrome (CFS). There were so many levels to this insidious complaint. Some suffering from ME just feel a bit tired but can maintain a normal lifestyle; others can be bedridden and need to be fed. Most days Ron was somewhere in the middle. Coming to terms with this was difficult for him. He often seemed depressed and felt he had let me down, as our hopes and dreams seemed to be put on hold. He struggled to make life as normal as he could and learned to pace himself between doing, resting and a little activity.

It was during this time that we were about to have another life-changing moment. My mother was strong, but a wonderfully kind lady and matriarch figure in our family. She was always there for us. The grandchildren adored her. She and my father put a gold thread of stability into the family and modelled good examples to us as children and the future generation.

We were all shaken to our roots when she announced that she had been ignoring a breast lump, but now there were significant changes to the lump. We made sure she was whisked off to her doctor, who promptly got her seen by a specialist. We ran to the Lord in prayer and knew we could trust Him whatever the outcome. Our worst nightmare was confirmed. She had breast cancer and would need a mastectomy as soon as possible.

Some years before my maternal grandmother, who still lived in Hull where Mum had lived as a child, had also been diagnosed with breast cancer. Mum would travel back and forth to Hull to support Grandma. My son was just one year old when she had a mastectomy, but sadly she died some years later. We have many happy memories of Florrie and my Grandad Arthur and I thank God for this lovely couple.

Mum made a good recovery following a total mastectomy, which involved a follow-up of radiotherapy, which did cause some burns but she hardly complained. She was very proud of her silicone prosthesis and her party piece, to our horror, was throwing it around for a game of catch! Mum was a brave lady and battled on enjoying her beloved family. We adored her fun ways and humour.

Some years later we noticed Mum wasn't quite herself; she seemed to have lost her spark. Then one day she went to sit on her chair at home and went down awkwardly. She ended up with a broken hip. Scans showed that sadly the cancer had gone into her bones and the prognosis was palliative treatment only. This meant that our local hospice, Tŷ Olwen, was now involved.

Mum went into the hospice for convalescing after she had the hip operation; this was our first experience of the hospice environment. What a blessing it was to us: friendly and kind, professional yet homely. Visiting was mostly all day so we made sure that Mum had lots of company. The children had great fun using her newly-acquired grabber stick by picking up small chocolates.

I remember one day a farmer who had been lambing came to visit his sick wife. The only way he could visit her was to bring a newly-born lamb that was orphaned with him, so he could feed and tend to the lamb as he visited his wife. I remember the delight on the nurses' faces as this little lamb just hours old went out in the gardens surrounding the hospice to have its first wee.

Mum came home with the support of the palliative day team in place, plus district nurses. They were all amazing support and I know we wouldn't have got through this time without them. She soldiered on, but we could see it was getting more and more difficult. She needed support. I helped with her personal hygiene and the household chores. I still had my bike and I would ride from Gorseinon to Penlan in no time. It was such a privilege to do that for her. I know Dad was very grateful for the help and family support.

11

LOVE IS KIND

We never forgot the kindness shown to us, particularly Babs and Richard who had so generously given Ron accommodation when he came to visit me from Leeds before we were married. We felt we could offer similar hospitality to others if there was a need.

A small fellowship from Neath came and visited us. We were talking with Jeff who told us that his girlfriend Pam from Reading was shortly coming to visit. We told him of the provision we were offering if needed. He thanked us and said he had everything arranged. Just two weeks later he rang to ask if he could take us up on the offer after all.

We were delighted and Pam arrived at Shalom2 to have bed and breakfast with us for a few days. We all immediately hit it off and felt like we had known each other for years; it was sweet fellowship together and we talked and prayed so much together.

Little did we know at the time the impact this meeting would have on our lives, and in fact the lives of many over the following years. Pam went home, then days later there was a thank-you card from her. As we opened it a cheque fell out. I hadn't got my glasses on so the print was somewhat blurred. I tried to focus on the cheque and thought it said £10. I put my glasses on and to my amazement the cheque wasn't for £10, but for £1,000! We were speechless. Pam went on to explain that she had never done anything like this before, but the Lord had impressed on her heart to do this for us.

We remained in shock for the rest of the weekend. We decided that we would use the money to pay off the two debts from Leeds that we were paying off weekly. One of these debts incurred by Ron was to provide a couple of his friends in Leeds with suits and wedding clothing. He was so generous.

We saw it as God using Pam to give us this amazing and wonderful gift which cleared both debts completely for us. Jehovah Jireh: the Lord will provide.

This was just the beginning of the way that the Lord used Pam in our lives and the lives of many of our friends. I will share her story in the following chapters.

Ron and I still hadn't found a church to settle in since he had come to live in Wales. We wanted to join the local Pentecostal church but were told there would be restrictions on us as we had been divorced and we wanted to serve the Lord freely.

We decided to start a church in the home. The people who came were those who wanted more of God and the Holy Spirit. We saw many wonderful answers to prayer and had sweet fellowship with one another as we praised God with the melodious sound of the guitar strumming out new choruses.

With great sadness after eighteen months it came to an abrupt end. I remember the awful feeling of hopelessness. I was reflecting on this and engulfed by the grief. I went into the garden looking but not focusing on anything except my pain of it all. Then suddenly, like it happened before, it's as if my eyes were taken to focus on a clump of daises growing in the grass and I sensed God say this, 'You see that clump of daises; you did not plant them...I did; you do not water them…I do; this will be like your life…though they are mowed down, they will grow again. You *will* be mowed down, and mowed down, *but* you *will* grow again and again and again.' Even though the disappointment was still very painful, I knew I would get over it, but only through God's love and provision.

When I am weak, He is strong

Still feeling battered and bruised and if I'm honest also a little discarded, I remember this particular day going up to my bedroom to pray for a lady called Lorna who was worryingly ill. She was having a lot of gastrointestinal problems and had been in great pain. She found she couldn't eat and was becoming very weak. Lorna could no longer concentrate and reading even had become impossible. She had shut herself off from all but her close family. We had been asked to pray for her. I felt helpless. I sat on the edge of the bed staring into space when my eye caught one of the hundreds of books on our shelves. It seemed to jump out at me! I was very curious and looked at the title, *Where Have You Gone, God?*

The Christian author and speaker was Jennifer Rees-Larcombe. I took it off the shelf and started to glance at the first pages. I knew instantly that this was the book for my very sick friend I had just been praying for. I read on and was even more convinced that she needed to read this book. How on earth could she, I thought, when she couldn't even eat or take anything in. I believe God popped the idea into my head. Record it! What a wonderful idea. I recorded it, knowing that she could be in control of how much she could take in, taking in snippets now and again like a little bird.

I knew this wasn't just a good idea but a 'God idea' and therefore couldn't fail. I sent off the recorded cassette blanketed with lots of prayers. Later that week I felt God saying, 'Tell her to drink milk.' I passed the message on and within three weeks of the spiritual medicine we had sent her from Jennifer's book and with the milk that she was now able to drink, Lorna began to make a remarkable recovery. Evidently, she had been taking anti-inflammatory drugs on an empty stomach and had damaged its lining. The milk she begun to drink helped her tummy recover slowly. She was back praising God again and being active in His Kingdom.

I was amazed at the way God had used us to help her. We weren't feeling particularly spiritual; we were still bathing the wounds from our hurt, yet God in His graciousness used the likes of us.

It didn't end there. I was so moved by what God had done and through the book, *Where Have You Gone, God?*, written by Jennifer Rees Larcombe who was a very sick lady at the time. I wanted to let her know how instrumental she had been in restoring Lorna. I wasn't even sure if Jennifer was still alive. Nevertheless, I wrote to her via the publisher, including a little picture I had made for her with pressed flowers and a Bible Scripture paraphrased from Job 23:10, *You shall come forth as gold.*

I was so surprised three weeks later when I had a reply. Jen was delighted with my letter and little picture. We bonded very quickly and for that period in her life I was able to journey with her. We wrote, spoke on the telephone and I was able to pray for her as she went on her speaking engagements medicated with morphine so that she could bear the pain she was in with the encephalitis she had contracted. Little did I know at the time that God had spoken to her and said that a stranger would come into her life and through her she would be healed. At first, she thought it was me. I was so glad that I didn't know all this at the time. We were in daily contact and I had the loveliest letters from her.

Just three months after our encounter, Jen was miraculously healed. Her book, *Unexpected Healing,* is well worth reading. Ron and I had the great honour of being her first staying guests at Tunbridge Wells. We also enjoyed subsequent visits to oversee her two youngest boys while they were away in Ireland on speaking engagements.

As I write this, I still marvel at the way God can use us in our weaknesses:

My grace is sufficient for you, for my power is made perfect in weakness. Therefore I will boast all the more gladly...in persecutions, in difficulties. For when I am weak, then I am strong (2 Corinthians 12:9-11, NIV).

What an encouragement for each one of us to keep pressing on through all the difficulties we encounter, knowing that when we are weak that's ok because then HE is strong. We cannot lose!

12

TRUST

Ron was an avid reader. He would impressively speed-read. The many Christian books he had brought with him were a testimony to this. He loved good solid doctrine and was very opposed to the wishy-washy 'gospel' that was coming in from America, nicknamed the 'health and wealth gospel'. Ron remained passionate about the true word of God throughout his life.

He had heard of a Christian bookshop in Gorseinon that did house calls on a book run, and he became a regular customer. Ron loved the fellowship with Byron and of course the chance to buy another book.

This was in the days before the internet and the availability we have now. They became close friends. Byron suggested that we could visit the church that he was involved with and part of the Mustard Seed bookshop. Ron laughed and said that he didn't know from one day to another with ME if he would be well enough. Byron confidently said, 'Well, come in your pyjamas then; we don't mind what you wear.' We decided to give it a go, took them up on the offer of a lift and arrived there and he didn't have to wear his pyjamas!

This was a significant part of our spiritual journey together. We enjoyed the church so much. I felt I had found my tribe. They were a loving bunch of people who cared for each other and shared in each other's lives. They modelled their Christianity on Acts 2. They lived in semi-community with extended families. We decided to settle in Calvary church.

After a while we were asked how we would feel about moving into the hub of the church community and become like a mum and dad for them. Did this mean we were on the move again? They knew our financial situation, so we suggested that they bought a house in the area and we would pay them rent. By the afternoon they had been in touch with a financial advisor and within days a mortgage could be arranged, and a deposit and all legal fees would be paid. We would have an interest-only mortgage which meant that while we couldn't work, we would be covered by Income Support as Ron still wasn't well enough to work. It was a nail-biting few weeks as we waited to see if this was God's will for us to move to Gorseinon. The Scripture that kept us going was Proverbs 3:5-6:

Trust in the LORD with all your heart and lean not on your own understanding; in all your ways submit to him, and he will make your paths straight.

We were over the moon when the news came through that everything had been approved and the mortgage granted. The house in question was next to the church's bookshop. The property was terraced with generously-sized rooms, as well as a garden and garage. One of the quirky things about the house was it had been tailor-made to suit its purpose. There was a door to a store cupboard under the stairs and because Brian, the owner of the house, also helped out in the Mustard Seed bookshop, they had taken part of the wall down and put another door in so that it was accessible for him to serve customers when they came into the shop.

The property was in need of some work but it was more than liveable. We were all very excited at this next chapter in our lives.

The move went well. As the last piece of furniture was being carried out by the removal men to their van, they experienced something very special. A sense of deep peace fell upon them. I felt it too and was able to explain that Jesus reigned in the home. It was as if He was leaving with us to abide with us in our new home - Shalom3.

Being such an organised person (slight OCD tendencies), I had the move working like a military operation. I would stay at the house in Trebanos with the removal men until it was emptied and I would clean the house before I left. Ron would be in charge of the furniture and boxes, etc. arriving in Gorseinon. Each box and piece was marked up into rooms designated for them. He could not go wrong, or so I thought.

When I arrived expecting it to be fairly sorted, I was greeted with the main room piled high to the ceiling with all the boxes. So much for my organisation! I remember doing something totally impractical - we cleared a gangway through the stacked high boxes in order to put my nana's old sewing machine, now my beloved desk, in its place of honour. Now I could carry on with the rest.

That night we managed to find our beds, have a meal and somewhere to sit, and over the next days we got everything shipshape. No sooner had we moved in that we started having people coming for help, sometimes well into night hours; the door was always open to anyone in need. It was a new way of living for us:

semi-community living. The new friends in the fellowship made us very welcome and loved. Community way of life was very new to us and took getting used to, but we loved it especially as we had an adorable young family, Pete, Cher and children, occupying the living accommodation behind the shop frontage. The novelty of being able to go next door to the Mustard Seed bookshop through the secret doorway under our stairs was great fun and continued for some years until we found out it was breaching fire regulations and finally had to have it bricked up for safety reasons.

Those early days were happy days in Calvary fellowship for us - so much fun. One warm sunny Sunday afternoon, Byron, who at the time lived with Pete and Cher at the Mustard Seed, decided to sunbathe on his treasured shiny motorbike. Catherine was with us for the day and we thought we would have a bit of fun and got a jug full of water and tipped it over the sunbathing Byron! A mistake! This turned into a full-time war and a water fight like no other. It was hilarious! Buckets and buckets came slopping out into the garden to be thrown over each other. Even the book van was involved to carry vessels of water to the war scene. Neighbours were in their gardens enjoying every minute.

A lady had arrived just before in deep distress and I had ushered her into the lounge and I was trying to talk with her with this commotion going on outside the door. I opened the door to chastise them and found Catherine grasping the stair spindles for her dear life as the plan was to take her fully clothed into the Mustard Seed house and put her into a prepared cold bath. I asked them to be quiet. I could hear through the crack of the door Catherine protesting with all her might... but in a whisper!

During these happy years in Calvary church, our family extended quite regularly. There was Adam, a Messianic Jew, who lived with our family for nearly six months and filled our house with colour! He was larger than life and loved his ministry in music. We loved learning about his culture and even had the privilege of having his dear mother from Tel Aviv stay with us for a holiday. An unforgettable memory of Adam was when he introduced Mark to raw chillies. We were having a meal and Adam added a handful of chillies to his dinner. Mark thought he'd do likewise. But after a visit to the bathroom decided he wouldn't do that again in a hurry!

When Jackie finished in Teen Challenge, she needed a temporary home and moved in with us for three months until moving on to another home in the fellowship. We were glad to provide rest and shelter for her especially when she was immobilised with phlebitis.

These were good times. Ron continued to battle with his health. The ME was a continuing struggle and to add to it he had type 2 diabetes, which meant he had to watch his diet. Ron was a wonderful cook and could conjure up a meal from practically anything. Our budget was tight but we always seemed to have enough to go around. Often we would start to prepare for the four of us, but by the end of the day with callers we could be up to eight or ten around the table. We loved the way the Lord always had enough in the pot to go around.

Ron had been told about a disability and renovation grant with Swansea City Council that he may have qualified for. Unusually for me, I was quite dismissive of it. I think I didn't want him to be disappointed if he was refused. He decided to apply, filled in the intricate forms and sent them off. Weeks went on and we had almost forgotten about it. Then a letter arrived to say he had been awarded the grant and would be visited by a person from the department who would check what work needed to be done to the house.

When the council employee arrived, he spent hours going through each part with a fine tooth-comb. His estimate was agreed by the council and he let us know that it would cost £24.000 with a grant of 100 per cent. We could not believe it. We knew when we had the survey done for the mortgage for Shalom3 that in time work would need to be done on the house. We knew we wouldn't be able to afford it, but we also knew that God wanted us to move there and we trusted Him with all that we would need. Still it was a shock to know how His provision would be given to us. His ways are beyond belief.

We found a builder who would take on the job of renovating our house. He told us that we would have to move out for about three months and that he would put us in an empty house in our road that he used for this purpose. This seemed ideal. We knew that new floors, replastering, a new roof and much more were being scheduled, so to have somewhere to live in the same vicinity was a blessing.

We were on the move again. We had to empty Shalom3 completely and we put our home in the hands of the builder. We made the best of our temporary accommodation but it was a difficult time. Because the council grant was paying for the work on the house, the builder wasn't very forthcoming with involving us and it did cause some tensions.

Mum's deteriorating health made things very emotional. I travelled most days to see to her needs and do the housework. There were tensions in the home with the stress of it all. We were all on a short fuse and mine was probably the shortest fuse of all, so best not to say anything more on that subject!

Finally, the house was finished. We had some issues with the standard of the builders' work, but we were so grateful to the council for the grant which made it all possible. Before we could move back into the house, it needed lots of TLC. There was rubble and dust to clean up. Our fellowship came out in force and took a room each. The walls were freshly plastered and ready for painting. All the curtain rails had to be replaced. The team of helpers were so busy cleaning, painting and drilling holes for new brackets to put up curtain rails. In no time it was looking more like a place to live, so we moved back in.

Within hours we had a phone call from a distressed friend and her husband who needed some support. We were aware that the house hadn't quite warmed up and to add to the problem the heating wasn't working properly. Our couple journeyed from the south of England in dense fog to be ministered to. They didn't mind the fact that the house was barely finished and went out completely different from the way they came in! And so it continued. What a privilege to be used that way.

13

LETTING GO

Mum wasn't well enough to come and see the work that had been done in the house but was always encouraged to hear all about what we were doing. I was spending more and more time helping my parents. Mum was definitely far from well. She spent much time in bed and was complaining about pain in her back. The Tŷ Olwen home care team upped her pain medication which helped a little.

Ron was wonderful to me and despite his physical weakness took charge of some of the household chores and released me to go whenever I wanted to be with my parents. This was such a blessing to me.

Dad had an appointment as an inpatient to have a cataract removed from one of his eyes. We decided the best thing was to get Mum into the hospice for respite while Dad was recovering, as they told him he couldn't bend after the operation until his eye had settled. I went with Mum by ambulance to Tŷ Olwen hospice. It didn't seem strange to her as she had had a period of convalescing there after her hip operation.

She settled in quickly but I saw a marked change in her. She had been suffering a lot of back pain over the previous months and her pain control had been managed. I knew she was in the best place for Dad to recover after his eye operation. I have a vivid memory of her lighting up her cigarette in bed and nearly dropping it on a few occasions. I spoke with the staff and we decided that for everyone's sake it was best that she didn't smoke.

She wasn't strong enough to go into a day room, her safety was paramount and we didn't want her to burn the hospice down. She became more confused. Scans were done and it showed metastases in her spine. The confusion could be a sign that it might have spread to other parts of the body. There was a rapid decline.

One of the senior doctors, Michael, was a personal friend of ours and from the church we attended. He kindly explained everything that was going on with Mum's medical condition. This helped me to be able to explain to the family. They lived very near the hospice and I knew they were praying for her and us as a family to be strengthened and comforted at this sad time.

I remember trying to pick the right moment to tell Dad who was recovering from his eye operation. I knew I couldn't keep it from him because we didn't know how long she had to live. I drove by moped the short journey from the hospice to his home and have to admit that when I arrived I broke down in floods of tears as I shared the bad news with him. He insisted on visiting that evening and said, 'I'm going to bend down to kiss her no matter what.'

On one visit a small choir arrived to sing carols. We sat beside Mum as they sang. I can't describe the sadness we felt. We looked up to see Michael, the devoted doctor, with tears in his eyes also. He knew his father in a different part of the UK was also terminally ill. There was a quiet stillness of mutual bonding I will never forget.

Each morning I went to Tŷ Olwen to sit beside her. The family joined me throughout the day as she got weaker and weaker. At least I knew she wasn't suffering any pain. Christmas decorations were decking the hospice but at home these were kept shut tightly in their boxes as celebration was the furthest thing in our hearts.

At the weekend I went in and she had become very sleepy and unresponsive. The staff prepared us for the ending. This lasted for 48 hours. The following day I was feeling so upset that before I went to visit her, I called at our dear friends' home, Michael the doctor and his wife Jane. I fell into their arms with grief; they hugged and hugged me, feeling my pain. They prayed, which so comforted me and I left for the short journey to the hospice. When I got there, I had the shock of my life! I'd prepared myself for 'the end' and there was Mum sitting up in bed chatting away. It took my breath away.

We had been given 'a window' as it was explained to me. Nobody could say how long. They told me it could be hours or even days and to enjoy this time that had been extended to her life.

Mum started to share with me how she had felt. 'I didn't know where I was and where I was going,' she said. (My heart's desire for Mum was eternal life and I had no reassurance of this.) I asked her if this made her scared. She replied it did. I continued with this conversation, asking her if she wanted to make sure where she would be going next. Her response was positive. I explained to her that she needed Jesus in her heart, to ask God to forgive her sins and to have the gift of eternal life. She smiled and said yes that's what she wanted…so I prayed this prayer…she prayed the best way she could and was at peace.

Just hours after she slipped into a coma and never spoke again. What a gift from God to give me this window for His gift of eternal life. Even in the middle of my grief was great joy. One afternoon my dad, sister and I sat in a single room with her as she came to the end of her time on earth. The end wasn't easy and I felt we needed to pray over her. My sister and I stood and placed our hands on her arms and simply asked God to take her from this decayed body and we released her into the hands of Jesus. We hadn't got to the 'amen' of the prayer and she had gone. Peace descended and we knew she was safe in the arms of Jesus.

December 14th, 1993. When Mum had left her home just two weeks before, we had no idea that God had plans for her ending. She was looked after like a queen in the hospice - all her needs were catered for 24/7. Her pain was controlled and we as a family had been given the opportunity to sit for hours on end knowing that she had all she needed, for which I am eternally grateful to God and the team at Tŷ Olwen hospice.

I stayed with Dad, helping with the necessary arrangements for the funeral. I kept a close eye on him as he grieved. He had taken over shopping duties sometime before, so this was something he could do easily. I remained his house cleaner, and he made regular day visits to us mid-week and to my sister's home on a Sunday. He continued to do this for years. I'm sure it helped him to fill the week and seeing someone most days which helped him tremendously.

14

COMFORT

Chris is one very special friend. She is generous beyond measure and spent many hours with me at the hospice bringing me treats to keep me going in the last weeks of Mum's life. Just six months after Mum's death Chris's dad had been diagnosed with cancer. His diagnosis was for palliative treatment only. He was taken into Tŷ Olwen and loved the day centre each week. He took up art and found the company and even fun so special at this time in his life as he became frailer.

He was admitted to Tŷ Olwen towards the end of his life. He was such a character. The staff loved him. One day when Chris was visiting him, his nurse hurried towards Chris as she entered his ward. She looked apprehensive and Chris thought it was bad news. Apparently when she was seeing to his personal hygiene that morning, she had accidentally shaved his moustache off! Chris was roaring with laughter and said kindly to her that it was ok even though it would have been the first time since he was a prisoner of war in Poland in the 1940s. I bet she didn't do that again in a hurry!

I was privileged to walk alongside Chris at this time, to provide support in a place that we had grown to love and could feel completely at home in. Chris was naturally worried about her dad's spiritual state. He had attended Bible studies, but his wartime experiences had caused a block with God.

He loved the fellowship he had in the home of the Harpers and particularly with May, a woman of great faith who lived with them. He would happily chat for hours with this dear elderly lady.

Chris spent many hours sitting beside her dad's bed silently praying for him, hoping that he would make his peace with God before the end of his life. Chris had stayed day and night at the hospice, but this particular day her husband Dorian had insisted she had a short break. Reluctantly she left the hospice for a very short time with her husband, who insisted he took her to a restaurant to eat something. It is one of the hardest things to do because you wonder if you will miss their departing and want to be with them till the end. Hurriedly she returned to find her dad peaceful and very pleased as he had had a visitor. May, who lived very near the hospice, felt led by God to go and talk with her friend, Glyn. God had truly sent her and before the end of her visit, he had repented of his sins and accepted Jesus as his Saviour.

Chris was ecstatic when she had a phone call from her son Kevin telling her of this. Her prayers were answered. In her heart of hearts she would have loved to have been there to experience what had happened. God knew there was a niggle in her heart to know that he really had become a Christian. The following day after May's visit to her dad, Chris woke in her makeshift chair bed beside him to the wafting fragrance of highly-perfumed flowers filling his room in the hospice…or so she thought. She popped her head out of the door, checked around the area, but no sign of any flowers; anyway, it was far too early for flower deliveries, she thought. Perhaps it was some expensive air freshener? There were no cleaners around at that time of the morning, so it wasn't that either. The fragrance was the strongest in his room and she knew there were no flowers or air freshener in there. Chris said there was such a strong beautiful fragrance with no flowers and no one had sprayed the room.

When Chris was ten years old, she was walking with a friend Cheryl in Port Eynon and went into the church. There was a small table with things like cones, nuts, flowers, etc. When she asked Cheryl about the table, she said they were gifts for Jesus. Chris wished they had something to give and decided to give the blackberries she had been collecting. They placed them on the table and started walking down the aisle. Then the singing started and Chris and Cheryl looked up into the roof as it sounded as if a choir of angels was there. God saw their giving and blessed them with this supernatural singing.

Every year around blackberry harvesting, Chris and Dorian her husband pick blackberries in different places, with containers overflowing, and Dorian turns them into wine.

God gives tenfold back when we give to Him

I knew none of this as it happened on that very early morning. I was praying for Chris and her dad in my home and was drawn to this Scripture for her:

Our lives are a Christ-like fragrance rising up to God. But this fragrance is perceived differently by those who are being saved and by those who are perishing. To those who are perishing, we are a dreadful smell of death and doom. But to those who are being saved, we are a life-giving perfume (2

Corinthians 2:15-17, NLT).

I shared this with Chris; it was like the last piece of the jigsaw and it all fell into place. She now had deep assurance that her father had been regenerated (John 3:3); he now had an eternal future and our awesome Heavenly Father had cared so much for Chris that He had allowed His fragrance to fill that little room where her frail father lay.

The morning after the beautiful fragrance was with her dad, Chris was sitting in his room in the hospice looking out of his window over the pond in the garden which was glistening in the sunlight (just like very bright sparkling diamonds). Then she suddenly heard a sound like tinkling bells and very quiet and beautiful singing. There was no one around. Again, God blessed Chris to hear angelic singing.

There was such a peace in the room which continued to his last day on earth. A few of us close to Chris were gathered in his room actually having our sandwiches and chatting quietly as her dad slept. We knew from our experience as volunteers there that it's important to keep that ambience around a sick and comatose patient, as the last sense to go is hearing.

Her dad was very peaceful and probably comforted to hear his beloved daughter talking and reminiscing about the wonderful times they had together. We were suddenly aware of the deepest peace descending on us, almost drawing us up heavenwards. We all went very quiet and looked at her dad. He had left us…gone to be with Jesus. His parting was something I will never forget as long as I live and count it a privilege to have been there beside Chris and her friends. We knew He had allowed us to experience her dad's passing and entry into life. Absent from the body…but present with the Lord.

15

HEALTH SCARES

Some months later, I had a breast check and a lump was found. I could never have imagined how it felt when a person's mortality is threatened. We take our health so much for granted. I must admit to being very scared due to the fact that my grandmother and mother died of breast cancer. Lots of praying took place. The lump was removed, a biopsy done and to my great relief the lump was benign.

Months later, another lump appeared on my other breast. This wasn't quite as scary but it needed to be removed. Once again, I was thanking God. The biopsy results showed that this lump was also benign. I could at last breathe out.

Our journey with God is like a rollercoaster. Our circumstances change with many family health issues to deal with and all the things that come to us to throw us off course, but He never once lets us down. He is with us every step of the way. Praise His Name!

Eighteen months after Mum's passing, I made enquiries about becoming a volunteer at the hospice. My friend Chris was also interested. During the time Mum was in the hospice, Chris had wonderfully supported me in practical ways, including bringing me sandwiches to make sure I was eating.

We were interviewed and we were taken on. At first, we were like petrified new students, but we soon settled into our roles and found it so rewarding. One of the things that delighted patients and staff on the Thursdays we were there was that we would bring in Chris's Victoria sandwich and my scones that we had baked. The patients would have our culinary delights for afternoon tea and the staff would grab a piece of cake or scone between their endless jobs.

Ron who was very gifted in catering, especially at preparing buffets, offered to prepare one for the staff in appreciation for all they did. It was a lot of work but was great fun, and we filled the Day Centre, which we had decorated with a certain theme and colour, and spread the tables with scrumptious delights.

The staff were so grateful and I'm sure it made them feel very special. This became a regular occurrence for our team of volunteers who worked so hard together to make these times possible.

**

It came as a great shock to hear that Hilary, my sister, had also found a breast lump. As soon as she was seen, they were very concerned and it was necessary for her to have a mastectomy because it was a cancerous lump. She also had quite a few lymph nodes removed. Hilary was a brave, strong-willed lady; she fought through and was soon up and about making sure she did her arm exercises to get the movement back in her arm again.

My nieces and her husband supported and encouraged her all the way. It was such a relief to see Hilary pick up the pieces and heal again, taking up a normal life for some years.

16

CATHERINE'S STORY

In our fellowship, we had a lovely Christian lady called June. Everyone knew and loved her. She was the community midwife for years and latterly worked in the ante-natal department in our local hospital. June's heart was for single pregnant ladies who found themselves in a crisis.

June helped set up a local pregnancy crisis centre which our church supported and she worked tirelessly with others with the same burden. In her role she met Catherine. Despite June seeing hundreds of pregnant women, many being single, Catherine's plight reached the centre of her heart.

Catherine was single with an unplanned pregnancy. This meant she would lose one of her jobs as a live-in part-time carer and the home that the job provided. She was doing this alone and was lost in hopelessness. It broke June's heart. She shared Catherine's plight confidentially with us and we prayed for her. One evening June felt led to bring Catherine around to meet us. Ron, whose heart was the biggest I have ever known, offered Catherine the opportunity to live with us. We didn't have a spare bedroom but we decided we could give her a reception room and make it into her own private bedroom and space. Catherine and June were so thrilled at the offer. Catherine wasn't going to be homeless after all. Her few personal belongings needed to be moved out of her accommodation quickly, so arrangements were made and she asked if we could store them in our garage while we got the room ready for her. We busily prepared the room so that she felt welcomed and wanted. Not long after Catherine moved in, we noticed such sadness in her face. She was pleased to be with us but her heart was empty and heavy; there was so much pain there.

Catherine fitted in like a glove on a hand and quickly became part of the family. We loved her like our own child. I have never had such a tidy home. Catherine would disappear quietly and before I knew it the dishes were washed, dried and put away, and my kitchen was sparkling. She worked hard in a nursing home each day until into late pregnancy.

Over the months we saw such a change in her. She began to trust us, asking us about our faith in Jesus, watching and experiencing our lifestyle as Christians spilling out into everyday acts of caring which we loved to do. Her grey-coloured life started to change. She started coming to church and very soon found the love of Jesus for herself. She was transformed and her life had hope and colour in it as never before. She was a new creation.

We started praying for Catherine to have her own home: a place to call her own. God answered in an amazing way and provided her with a three-bedroomed modern house, with a new kitchen and bathroom on a private estate. The local council was her landlord. We were ecstatic! Even the fact that she had no furniture to put in it didn't deter us. We both knew from our own personal experience what it was to be homeless and that God always does provide everything abundantly. We put out an SOS request to the fellowship, friends and family and Catherine moved in with all she could ever need.

Isn't this what true Christianity should be all about? When there is a need, should we just sit there and say, 'Well, God bless you.' Or should we offer them our best. You need a chair. Come, choose which one of mine you want! In my experience there is no greater joy than to do just this. God loves a cheerful giver.

June had been away on holiday when the house was offered to Catherine and we furnished it. It was a sheer delight to surprise June on her return to take her on a mystery trip, to ring a door bell of a house she didn't know and to see the occupant opening the door being her very own Catherine. It was priceless!

Not long after this, Catherine's baby was born - a beautiful little girl called Elizabeth - and we had the joy of being present at the birth. Catherine eventually met a wonderful man in our fellowship called Mike. To this day they are blissfully happy together praising God for each other and all He has done for them. Faithful, wonderful God!

We had been in Calvary some years, living in our own home with our own purse but we were very much a community church. We cared for one another in depth that I have yet to find again. But we have an enemy who hates to see Christians sharing the gospel and growing in numbers. Sadly, our season ended abruptly. There were many reasons but we experienced the horrible time when a fellowship falls apart. It was a hugely devastating time for us and for so many. It took years for many to have the courage to venture into another church and begin fellowshipping again.

Eventually we settled in a local church. It was small, safe and friendly.

17

RON'S BIG 'C' JOURNEY

We had no sooner gathered ourselves together after the shock of Hilary's breast cancer when I noticed Ron began having what we thought was indigestion.

He saw our GP who tried various medications, but nothing made any difference. He noticed that after he had eaten, he felt the food had become stuck in his gullet. It was very unpleasant for him. The doctor decided he needed to be referred for a scan. The appointment came very quickly and with apprehension we attended.

The test was done and they calmly asked him to attend for a scan on the same day in another hospital. When we arrived, they were waiting for us. Strange I thought - this was like private treatment. I began to feel a little suspicious. We were ushered into the scanning room and when the scan was completed, they told us straightaway that they had discovered a lump on the oesophagus, which could be a polyp. A biopsy was taken, he would need further investigations and would see a specialist.

Ron seemed very low-key about it and I think was pleased to know what was seemingly causing the swallowing problems. I, however, had a gut feeling that there was something more. Over these past years attending many oncology appointments with Mum, I saw how they broke the bad news, often giving only a little information at a time. I expect it was for the shock not to be overwhelming.

Professor Baxter was assigned as Ron's specialist who saw us very soon after the scan. I remember it was my birthday and my family were home on holiday from Germany and we had planned a celebration buffet at home that evening. As Ron and I sat in Professor Baxter's consulting room waiting for the full diagnosis, all sorts of things were going through my mind. The 'what ifs' threatened to overwhelm me.

Professor Baxter was a great man. He was straight in his manner but so approachable. He didn't mince his words and told Ron that what had first been thought to be a polyp, was in fact oesophageal cancer. The words hit us like a bolt of lightning. Surely not…not the big 'C'? He hadn't drunk or smoked for years; they must have got it wrong. He gently assured us that the scan was correct and proceeded to tell us the course of action. The good news was that it hadn't spread through the walls of the oesophagus.

There would be an operation which meant going into the oesophagus to remove the cancerous lump. He made it sound so easy, like taking out a tooth. But first he would need a combination treatment of chemotherapy and radiotherapy which would be quite intense.

We left the hospital in shock with this awful news. Ron was determined to go ahead with the evening's planned celebration. We decided not to tell anyone that evening, so we put on the biggest masks we could, smiling, laughing and enjoying the evening, when in fact our tummies were in knots and our hearts as heavy as lead as we dreaded what may lay ahead, but we never doubted that God was with us every step of the way.

We entered the world of oncology. I say 'we' because when someone dear to you gets hit by a serious disease, you enter into it with them. The empathy and ability to feel part of their sufferings is surely a gift from God as we share in their sufferings.

The multidisciplinary team met to discuss Ron's case and a plan of action was to be put in place. He started as an in-patient in the Oncology Ward at Singleton hospital. He was scheduled to have a combination of intravenous chemotherapy alongside a regime of radiotherapy which would target the lower third of his oesophagus where the growth was located. The combination of the two treatments given simultaneously was quite a new thing. We knew that the chemo drugs were going to be aggressive. I remember being told by a nurse that she had noticed if a chemo drug was orange then her patients usually lost their hair; so we were prepared beforehand.

The treatment was very unpleasant and as time went on, he was finding eating more difficult. The chemo often changes the taste of foods and they can taste 'tinny'. One day he said he just had to have steak and chips! This was a surprise as he barely fancied food. I went to the local pub and brought out what he had asked for - steak and chips! It took him hours to eat even a small proportion, but he loved every mouthful. The staff kindly heated it in a microwave. The other patients were commenting on the lovely aroma coming from the kitchen which made them hungry - not quite like hospital food!

As Ron's treatment progressed it became more and more difficult for him to swallow and he had to have puréed foods.

In the ward Ron was known as 'the Vicar'. His Bible would sit proudly on his locker and despite the nausea and tiredness that engulfs you during such treatment he would wheel his stand that held the chemo drug and share his faith in Jesus to anyone who would want to hear. He was not ever ashamed of the gospel and lived by the Scripture:

For I am not ashamed of the gospel, because it is the power of God that brings salvation to everyone who believes (Romans 1:16 NIV).

Believing this with all his heart, he was like an evangelist. His kind and gentle heart drew people. One frightened elderly man talked for hours with Ron who comforted him and led him to the love of Jesus, and his fears of the unknown left him. There were many lives he touched in the hospital ward. We rejoiced that out of bad, God was bringing good.

Ron came home exhausted after the treatment and rested most of each day. I remember coming back from church and he was trying to eat some dinner. Every time he put his head down to eat, some hair would fall out onto the plate. He had had enough! He looked at me and said, 'let's get this hair shaved off!' So that's what I did. Fortunately, shaved heads, thanks to David Beckham, were fashionable, so it wasn't too traumatic.

The next stage was to rescan the growth to see if it had shrunk enough for the operation. Professor Baxter was pleased with the results and scheduled the operation to remove it. It's a good job he didn't give us details of this when we were first told of his cancer. He explained in detail what he was going to do. How we wished it was like the board game *Operation* where you just picked out the part you wanted! Prof. Baxter, as he was affectionately known, proceeded to tell us that this was a long operation called an 'open oesophagectomy'.

He would remove part of the oesophagus and any surrounding tissues to make sure he had all the cancer. After it was removed, the oesophagus would be rebuilt from part of the stomach and joined back together. The operation has been known to last for up to twelve hours, but he spared us from the finer details.

Prof. was very cool and confident that this was quite normal for him and instilled confidence into Ron. He trusted him implicitly but trusted Jesus more, knowing his times were safe in His hands; nobody could shorten them or lengthen them. So he knew he was safe and in complete peace about the operation.

The day of the operation arrived. Ron had been taken into the ward the day before for pre-assessments. The staff had kindly agreed for me to be allowed to be with Ron before he went down to theatre. That was such a comfort for us both as we were able to pray together and I could sit quietly holding his hand and bringing him comfort. They even allowed me to go into the ante-theatre just before an epidural and general anaesthetic were given. I kissed him goodbye and left him in the total trust of God, Prof. and his team.

My lovely friends had asked me what I wanted to do while Ron was in theatre. I insisted I wanted to be in and near the hospital, so I chose to spend some of the time in Tŷ Olwen hospice's tea bar. Tŷ Olwen is situated in the grounds of Morriston Hospital. I wanted to go there as I loved it there and it felt like home as we had become part of the team through our volunteering on the wards. I sat in the tea bar with the lovely company of my friends for some hours drinking copious mugs of tea. As some of the staff passed by, they would come up to my chair and give me a squeeze or gentle hug…words weren't needed.

Lunchtime came, a picnic had been made for me and I was whisked away to the nearby reservoir that I loved so much. It was wonderful having such precious company during the time while Ron was being operated on. We returned to the hospital and continued drinking tea.

I was told to contact the ward about 4.00p.m. that afternoon to find out the progress of Ron's operation that had started not long after 8.00a.m. I rang the ward and they said he was still in theatre and asked me to ring back in one hour.

For the first time that day the time started to drag. More tea, more talk. Chris was staying on with me until Ron had come out of theatre. Five o'clock arrived and I eagerly contacted the ward to be told again that Ron was still in theatre. I had butterflies in my stomach and started to worry. The 'what ifs' started to bombard my mind and the peace I had been surrounded by started to wane. I silently chastised myself, remembering that the operation could take up to twelve hours to complete.

Surely though I would hear at 6.00p.m. when I rang the ward again. Six o'clock arrived and I rang the ward, but Ron was still in theatre. Should I ring back at seven? I knew I couldn't drink any more tea - I was waterlogged and we were talked out!

It was just after 6.00p.m. when Chris and I settled in the hospital dining room, overlooking the morgue to be precise. What happened next was nothing short of a miracle.

I remember we were both tired out from incessantly chatting all day, so we sat quietly. I was trying not to be anxious. It was nearly eleven hours since Ron's operation had started. It's difficult to describe what happened in words because it was something quite supernatural. We didn't go to sleep. We both had exactly the same experience. It was as if we had been anaesthetised. We were totally unaware that we had lost nearly one hour. I felt completely refreshed, strengthened and full of His peace, as did Chris. We shook our heads in amazement. What had happened? We knew we hadn't slept. We were in a busy hospital dining area. I checked my watch; it was just a few minutes short of 7.00p.m., the time I was to ring the ward again. We got up quickly, still in awe of what God had done.

We hastily walked along the corridor passing the operating theatres on the way to the ward. I was saying to Chris that I wondered how Ron's operation had gone. With that, the person in front of me wearing operating scrubs turned back and stopped me to ask if I was Mrs Williams. He went on to say that he was the anaesthetist for the whole of the operation and gave me a detailed account of all that had happened, and it had gone very well. He had just taken Ron into Intensive Care and I could visit him in half-an-hour. We were gobsmacked!

God had taken an hour away from us so that I didn't have to go through any more painful waiting. He orchestrated that as we hastily walked the corridor towards the ward, we would 'just happen' to bump into a member of the operating team as he had left Ron to the care of ITU, and then did the most unusual thing by sharing with me all that had happened in the operation. Don't ask me how He did; I will never know. But I can, as can Chris, declare the authenticity of this awesome happening. I felt I had been literally hugged by God with His never-ending love and concern. What a day to remember!

Thirty minutes later I went to be with Ron in ITU. I was shocked when I saw him and wasn't prepared to see him looking like 'the Hulk'. He was twice the size! I learned after that his tissues were full of water which was all part of the operation he had undergone. There were wires and pipes everywhere. He wasn't fully conscious but he hadn't needed the life support machine as he first thought he would: all good signs. When I knew he was settled and would sleep for some time, I left exhausted but praising God from the rooftops for bringing Ron safely through the operation and all that He had done for me that day.

Ron spent a few days in Intensive Care, did very well and was moved onto the High Dependency Unit and finally back onto the ward. I was shocked to see the evidence of his operation when I saw his neatly-stitched incision. It ran from his sternum, around his rib cage, around to the back of the spine and up to his shoulder blade. Internally his stomach was changed as they had removed part of the oesophagus and used part of his stomach to join it together again. It was a huge operation and we knew it was going to take time to recover and heal again.

Towards the end of the week, with Ron having lived mostly on fluids, the doctor came and asked him how he was coping with eating. Ron was delighted to say that he had been given fish and chips which he thoroughly enjoyed! The doctor's eyes nearly popped out of his head on hearing this and asked Ron how he was feeling after he had eaten it. Ron, unaware of the doctor's concern, said, 'I was fine.' Evidently it was a little too soon to eat such things. Apparently, it proved his new oesophagus was working very well! For some time he had to be in a single room as he had contracted the hospital bug, MRSA. It was a blessing in disguise as he was in an en-suite room and had some quality sleep.

There was quite a trauma on the body and the mind too. I remember the doctor warning me that he would need time to adjust and to keep everything calm and peaceful without any changes. The calm and peaceful bit I was ok with, but the changes could have caused a problem because when Ron was in hospital I had stencilled daisies all over the kitchen ceiling! When he came home and walked through the kitchen at a snail's pace because of the weakness, he gazed up, saw the stencilled daises all over the ceiling and quietly said, 'Nice,' and walked back into the lounge again. What a relief!

The healing was a slow process and having the ME slowed it up. His stitches were taken out and this made mobility a bit easier and helped the massive scar heal. There was just one tiny area giving him trouble and that was the only thing he complained about. It was near the shoulder blades and was causing him so much distress.

We finally decided to see the doctor in the hospital who was very pleased at the healing to date. But Ron insisted that something wasn't right between his shoulder blades. On close inspection, they found an external stitch which had turned in, probably caught a nerve ending and the skin had grown over it. Poor old Ron; no wonder it was so uncomfortable. They cut it out and the relief was immediate. Weeks turned into months; he was eating normally again and enjoying life.

18

EXTRA TIME

During Ron's convalescence we were invited to Dr Michael and Jane's new home in a community called Burrswood Health and Wellbeing Centre where he had taken up a post as senior doctor. What a wonderful place where Ron could convalesce. We were looked after amazingly.

Michael's face was a picture when we had our first meal with them. He could not believe how Ron could successfully eat such a quantity with only a bit of a stomach left. He chuckled for hours with disbelief of what he had witnessed. We were wrapped in TLC by this dear couple and went home thoroughly refreshed, thanks to them. How rich we are to have beautiful God-given friends to walk beside us on our journey here on earth.

Some young friends had invited us to their wedding in Elgin, midway between Inverness and Aberdeen in Scotland. Ron set himself a goal for us to attend. I was astonished and quite honestly thought this was unachievable because of the distance in miles. He said we would travel by National Express coach and it would take around twelve hours. As the date drew nearer, he was even more determined.

We set off for bonny Scotland. I have to admit it was a beautiful journey especially as we crossed the border into the rough terrain of Scotland. Ron didn't complain once during the long journey. In fact, I was the one who wriggled and groaned in my seat with sciatica. What an achievement for him. I was so proud of him making such an effort, but the rewards he had far outweighed the discomforts he may have felt.

The wedding and the time we spent with friends was etched into our memories for ever. To have goals to stretch when you are fighting cancer enriches your life. You get to jump off the treadmill of life and take time to smell the roses and appreciate what the Creator has given you in a new and deeper way. Ron most certainly did this.

19

PREPARATION FOR HEAVEN

For a couple of years Ron continued doing well and having regular check-ups. He had some pain which was checked on and it was discovered that the cancer had metastasised to the liver.

Ron's oncologist suggested more chemotherapy. It was a hard decision for him. I wanted him to fight it and was glad when he agreed to have the treatment. It was a very hard regime, but he got through it.

They needed him to have a second course of chemotherapy, which he started, but he became so ill and nearly died, so it was stopped. His quality of life was being impaired. He was told that his condition was terminal and the treatment would be palliative. There was no cure. We prayed hard about this and he decided, with me being in total agreement, to choose quality of life over quantity.

I can only describe the time that we had left together as a wonderful journey as he approached eternal life with Jesus. We had a wonderful summer. It was as if I had entered into his world. Although he became tired very quickly and spent a lot of time resting and sleeping, he was in total peace.

The quality he had in those last months of his life was second to none. The pace was slow and achievable and most of all flexible. We had the sense of God being with us every step of the way. The GP surgery was so supportive, as was the Tŷ Olwen team, and his pain levels were well controlled with their expert help.

So many Christians will only accept the teaching of 'healing now' and miss out on the final chapter of the lives of their dear ones they journey with. In my experience I have seen many almost lose their faith because of this teaching that everyone has to be healed and if you aren't then there's something wrong in your life and there must be sin stopping your healing.

It is wise to allow God to speak to you and see if He is showing you anything He wants to highlight and free you from, but at the end of the day it's up to Him. He may heal, He may not. I totally believe that complete healing can sometimes only take place when we are reunited with Him.

To have missed this final season of Ron's life by nagging God, being angry and discontent, and losing that peace that passes all understanding would have been unthinkable. This was a bitter-sweet time: not always easy, but it contained a joy that doesn't come from this world, but from God alone.

Ron was increasingly unwell and very tired by this point. One of my fond memories of him was how his thoughtfulness never ever left him, despite fighting a losing battle with the cancer.

This particular day he had spent most of the time in bed. It was late evening and he knew that one of the things I hated doing, and had a bit of a thing about, was checking that everything was turned off before I retired to bed myself. I had just started doing this ritual in the kitchen when I heard the stairs creaking and I saw him making his way down towards me in his blue pyjamas and emerald-green dressing gown. He insisted that he should help me. On the way to the kitchen we decided to do a rather slow but fun Cuban conga carnival dance through the hallway. It was good to hear him laugh as we did something silly together at such a serious and sad time.

The doctor came some days later. He could see he was struggling and decided to put him on steroids. Ron gave me strict instructions that no matter who came to visit him he didn't want to be disturbed. This was very unlike him, but I think he felt so ill and exhausted that even talking and listening was too much. He settled down having taken his new medication and I continued with my chores around the house checking on him periodically.

In the afternoon my stepson Mark arrived. Mark and I had many challenging years together and during this difficult time we had struggles with our relationship. I knew I had to honour Ron's wish not to be disturbed by anyone. We sat with a cup of tea and started to talk.

What happened next was so healing for our relationship. It was as if the Holy Spirit fell on us and we started talking deeply as we laid our hearts before each other in honesty and truth. We cried and forgave one another for our misunderstandings and ended up hugging each other with a new love in our hearts that can only have been given by God.

I felt led to say to Mark that perhaps he could just pop upstairs to see his dad for a short visit, or if he was asleep to let him continue sleeping. Mark came downstairs saying his dad was asleep, but he was so glad to have seen him. He left a different young man. I was so very grateful to God for the work he had done on my heart and Mark's, and also for the prompt, despite Ron's instructions, to let Mark see his dad. This was the last time he saw his precious father.

All day I was aware of a stillness and a deep peace permeating our home. As early evening approached, I heard Ron call out that he felt that he had turned a corner. I was pleased to hear this. He reminded me that my favourite programme would soon be on the television. I asked him if he felt like eating and he wanted toast and tea.

As I was preparing this, I heard a noise coming from the bathroom above me. I quickly went upstairs to see what had happened. Ron had got to the bathroom but on the way back into the bedroom he had collapsed on the easy chair in the bedroom. He could speak, but beckoned to me that he wanted to get back into bed. I knew I couldn't lift him on my own, but he kept pointing to the bed. The next thing, he is IN the bed! I know I didn't lift him; I also know that he couldn't move an inch, but he was 'moved' into the bed. I didn't see anyone but I knew that there must have been an angel present to lift Ron safely into the bed. He was sitting up and had been a little sick.

I held him in my arms reassuring and comforting him. He gasped and the Lord took him. His struggle was over. I just stayed there for a few minutes, not knowing what to do; it had all happened so quickly.

Just half-an-hour earlier he had said he felt he'd turned a corner. I thought he'd meant he was feeling better. The 'corner' must have been his nearness to heaven. I rang the emergency services to tell them what had happened. Even though there was an ambulance depot in our street, there were no vehicles available and one would have to come from Ammanford which is quite a distance from where we lived. As I waited for the ambulance to arrive, I held him in my arms and had a sense of deep gratitude to God for the way He had allowed his passing to be dignified, and allowed him to remain of sound mind right to the end.

The ambulance arrived, as well as the police as it was a sudden death, and they asked me if I wanted them to resuscitate. I was so glad I had had the conversation with Ron months before when I casually asked him how he would feel about resuscitation. He was adamant he would not want it, so my decision to say no to resuscitation wasn't a difficult one for me. I was so glad as I knew his ribs had become very brittle after the radiotherapy and often if he coughed heavily, he felt as if they would crack. I was saved that trauma.

I'm not sure that the emergency services knew what to make of me. I was still full of gratitude and in awe of what God had done in those few hours. Because Ron had seen the GP that morning the decision was made that there was no need for a post-mortem.

My very close friend Caren came to support me, and Gareth also arrived. Before he had become a pastor, Gareth was a trained nurse, so he laid Ron out with dignity and sensitivity. God had got everything in hand for me.

The family had arrived to help me make the funeral arrangements. The church at Penyrheol was wonderful, accommodating me with every request I made for the service to celebrate Ron's life. They were even going to serve and provide the refreshments after the burial. The sense of peace and His presence were almost tangible, especially in the dining room - it was so powerfully strong that we could not even stand up and had to sit down!

December 2nd, 2000 arrived with many friends and family from afar. It had been a very wet week and the forecast was for sun and rain, so I prayed for a rainbow. Was that a selfish prayer? Maybe, but the Lord knew how much this meant to me.

The service at church went very well and as the coffin was being processed out from the church Ron's young friend Reuben, who has Down's syndrome, unreservedly stood on his seat and in a loud voice shouted out, 'Love you Ron,' and openly wept. There wasn't a dry eye in the church and we made our way over to the cemetery. As I was getting out of the mourners' car, the biggest and best rainbow ever appeared in the sky, the bow earthing itself in the cemetery.

Most people knew of my prayer request and probably thought I was a bit over the top to ask for such a thing, but here it was so large and bright, my heart was bursting with thanks to Him. He knows how precious rainbows are to me and here was one on this significant day, like my baptism, like my engagement to Ron, and now the day Ron was put to rest. Ron's family from London whom I had only met on a few occasions were in awe. I paid my last respects to my God-given husband and even as I began to walk away from his grave, they were persistently asking me about the life we had with Jesus.

The very next day in my daily readings was this quote from *Streams in the Desert: 366 Daily*

Devotional Readings by Jim Reimann, L. B. E. Cowman:

Be strong, my soul! Your loved ones go within the veil. God's yours, e'en so; be strong. be strong, my soul! Death looms in view. Lo, hear your God! He'll bear you through; be strong. E'en for the dead I will not bind my soul to grief; death cannot long divide. For is it not as though the rose that climbed my garden wall has blossomed on the other side? Death does hide, but not divide; you are but on Christ's other side! You are with Christ, and Christ with me; in Christ united still are we.

Henry Ward Beecher

Praise and deep gratitude welled up in my heart; my loving compassionate Saviour was speaking to me through these words written many decades before, yet they were like the oil of Gilead to my soul washing over me with His love and kindness.

How providential that I should be writing this chapter of Ron's final weeks on this earth on the anniversary of his passing. My heart is warmed by the comments on social media where I had put a picture of Ron that his son Mark had beautifully sketched. This led to a flurry of kind messages of their memories of this dear man.

Here are just two:

Aw, that face brought such memories back. An angel of a man, made a huge difference to me, never ever forgotten... Lorraine King

I remember him with joy and thankfulness - happy memories... Dr Michael Harper

The next days and weeks were a bit of a blur. I can never thank friends enough like Caren who walked so closely during this journey. Friends had stayed with me for company to help me through those difficult, dark winter days. Christmas came and went. Strange as this may sound, the deep joy in my heart that Ron was out of pain and in heaven praising his Saviour brought me immense comfort. It shone through any grief I felt and numbed the pain.

The **seven** emotional **stages of grief** are understood to be shock or disbelief, denial, bargaining, guilt, anger, depression, and acceptance/hope. Symptoms of **grief** can be emotional, physical, social or religious in nature, but it is my experience that it is individual and unique for each person and not always in this order. Each person has the right to grieve the way they need to.

The reality of dear Ron no longer being with me was often quite overwhelming and scary, but I clung onto the Lord tightly.

The money side of things was always handled by Ron. Now I was back at the helm to manage finances once again. He managed a very small income incredibly well. He helped many to handle their debts and get solvent again. Just before Ron was diagnosed with cancer, he and our financial advisor had changed the mortgage to an endowment mortgage. When we took on Shalom3 in Gorseinon we knew we would never own the house as we paid only the interest. However, because the mortgage was changed, it meant if one of us died, the house would automatically go to the remaining spouse. So I now owned my home. God moves in mysterious ways!

One of the hardest things for me was getting used to living on my own. This was the first time in my life. Some days I would feel like I was rattling around the house.

I began to take up my volunteer work as the new year came and this helped me to have a purpose. Coming home often in the dark to an empty house was not easy. But I found a solution that worked for me. I put the hall light on a timer so it was more inviting to come home to. I knew that God says He would never leave me or forsake me, so each time I unlocked my front door and got into the porch I would speak out 'I'm home, Jesus.' I always hoped that there was nobody around otherwise they might think I'd lost it! This worked perfectly for me. I learnt over time to do things on my own and as the months moved on my confidence grew. I was on my own but never alone. He was with me every second of the day.

I missed Ron for some of the silliest things. One was my earrings. I was forever losing one or the backs would disappear on the floor or carpet. Poor God had to put up with me one day ranting and raving at Him because he'd taken Ron from me and I angrily asked him who would find the back of my earrings now! Then I sobbed like a baby…one way for the grief to come out. When I think back to how trivial this was, but it wasn't to God. He understood my anger, my unreasonable reaction. His response to this was whenever I lost an earring or the back of it, as I started looking it was as if He would fix my eyes on the area where it lay: unbelievable…yes…but that's exactly what happened!

20

TRINIDAD AND TOBAGO

I set a plan for family and friends to take my place in seeing to Dad's needs while I went on our exotic holiday. I had been overseeing him since Mum's passing with the help of my sister. My daughter had suggested we had a holiday in a sunny part of the world after the grey and damp winter we had experienced. I remembered the offer we had from a young vet friend at church inviting me to stay with her family. I even surprised myself by saying we are coming! The holiday was a wonderful experience.

We stayed with our friends in Trinidad in the West Indies with some days on the island of beautiful Tobago. We left the UK in its gloomy grey winter to the friendly, vibrant colourful people of the Caribbean with its turquoise seas, blue skies, hot sun and stunning white sandy beaches.

I loved every minute of it, especially early mornings when I would go to the sea edge to have a quiet time with the Lord and watch the children throw crumbs of bread into the water and see the most beautiful coloured fish rise to the surface to devour the breadcrumbs, to the delight of us onlookers. I found this paradise a superb place to reflect over the past months and to begin the healing process. It truly was a gift from God.

I saw this wonderful experience as a part of heaven for me. A gift for me from God in my bereavement. Those of you who have experienced the darkness of loss will know that it is a time of heartache, and facing

Sue Williams

an unknown future can be very scary. Yet having the very presence of Jesus in your life, in your heart, cushions the pain and propels you to embrace the future and all He has in it for you. It is over nineteen years since this holiday in paradise yet I can recall its beauty, and the memories bring warmth to my soul. I am eternally grateful to God for taking me there and introducing me to the extravagance of His creation in this part of His world.

Just three weeks after my return, Dad's health started to decline. He was very sick and was admitted to hospital with heart failure and diabetes. The family were all very worried about him, but after three weeks he made a remarkable recovery and was discharged with a new regime of medication.

He was soon able to live independently with just my overseeing him and cleaning for him, and he returned to his regular weekly full-day visits to me and to my sister and family where he was well fed and had a 'doggie bag' to take home for the next day. We were able to stay on this plateau for quite some time and it worked successfully.

136

21

NICHOLASTON HOUSE
AND PARKLANDS CHURCH

I became involved with a beautiful retreat centre in Nicholaston, Gower. The setting was spectacular, overlooking the coastline of Oxwich bay. Ron and I had stayed there the previous year for his last birthday on this earth. What a wonderful gift for us!

I felt led by God to become part of this organisation where hearts were healed, people set free by the help they received in this place of peace. It was running with my vision and I was amazed. I spoke with my church leader about my desire to be part of the work of Nicholaston House, but sadly they didn't feel they could support my involvement. I knew I had to make a choice.

When walking with the Lord sometimes we have to make a stand which isn't popular and not always understood. That was the case in this instance. I thanked them for the years that I had fellowshipped with lovely folks there but felt so strongly I had to obey what I believed the Lord was asking of me.

The members of the church were lovely people, but I knew to many of them I was like a square peg in a round hole. I was a charismatic, born-again, spirit-filled lady who probably would be more suited to a Pentecostal contemporary worship style. I said my goodbyes and thanks to them and left sad in some ways, but I believed in faith that this was God's will for my life.

I immediately looked for a church that supported the work of Nicholaston House. I was told that Parklands church was very connected with the retreat home and supported their work wholeheartedly. I went along and fitted in like a hand in a glove.

It was a city church that catered for students with their varied congregation. I spoke with the pastor and told him the reasons I had left my church in Penyrheol. He stood by my decision and welcomed me to the family of Parklands.

I settled in very quickly. My heart has always been pastoral. I just love people, and in no time I was getting involved. I joined a home group which met each week. It was wonderful to bond and relate closely to these folks and our faith grew through our Bible studies and sharing times.

I loved the dynamics and diversity of the church set in contemporary worship. I marvelled at the way it accommodated people with varying viewpoints without the usual church fall outs that I had experienced in the past. I soon realised that God had led me to Parklands for His plan and a purpose, not just to find a church that supported the work of Nicholaston House.

My time in Nicholaston was very precious. It started with attending the monthly Sunday praise evenings. There was such a presence of God in these meetings. We prayed for the needs of the house and very quickly I became part of its community. A course for prayer ministry became available which I found invaluable and a great asset for future ministry. I started helping on Mondays when the volunteers worked in the house and enjoyed a shared lunch and wonderful fellowship.

I met Helena Wilkinson who worked and lived in the house. She has an amazing ministry in eating disorders. Helena is an author and international speaker. She herself had been anorexic and understood perfectly the devastating effect eating disorders can have on a life. We became very good friends.

When an extension was being built at Nicholaston, Helena needed somewhere to live, so I offered her a home with me at Shalom3. It was quite a culture shock, coming from the tranquillity of Gower to living on a main road with its bustling traffic. It was such a good time for both of us. After eight months the extension was ready for her to move back to Nicholaston and I had the privilege of helping her set up home in her new 'penthouse' pad. We decided it made sense for me to go each Sunday afternoon and stay at Helena's apartment. This way I could help with the work there.

The time I spent in Nicholaston House was so beneficial for me and a real learning curve. I learnt so much which helped me in future pastoral work and spiritually because of the input I received. There were some challenging and even painful times, but I grew through them, as did we all.

Being a carer for my late husband and Dad's needs for more help increasing, I saw the need to care for the carers. I set up a biannual day set aside for carers. We ran them for almost twelve years. We would have a different speaker each time, beautiful worship and a time for personal prayer and reflection. Each day we held was inhabited by God in such wonderful ways. The people who attended would often say that they felt as if they'd been on a week's holiday. God knew exactly what each person needed and He would bless them abundantly. I actually hoped that one day I would serve Him there and live as part of their community. God had other ideas!

22

WITH THIS RING I THEE WED

As the months rolled on and grief was taking its course, I could see that I was more than surviving - I was actually living each day to its fullness.

I have never liked sitting doing nothing so my overseeing caring role for Dad was jogging along nicely. My volunteer work filled a huge part of my week. In fact, everything was ticking over nicely.

It must have been nearly three years since Ron's passing and I was having a quiet time with the Lord. For a while I had wondered what my future was going to be; was I to remain single? If so, I was quite happy with that. I felt that the Holy Spirit took me to this passage in Isaiah 54:5:

For your Maker is your husband - the LORD Almighty is His name - the Holy One of Israel is your Redeemer; He is called the God of all the earth.

I had always had great comfort from this Scripture, knew it well and applied it to my life. I thanked Him and carried on with my quiet time. Again and again the Scripture kept repeating in my mind, but it was being personalised - 'I AM your husband'. Just like He had done those years before when He repeatedly spoke to me for forty-eight hours about being baptised, I kept hearing the same words over and over again: 'I AM your husband...I AM your husband.' I must admit to being a little frustrated as I would repeat, 'Yes, yes, I know,' but it was as if I was missing something! I took time to reflect and see if I could perceive what I was missing. Yes, I knew He was my husband so what did He want me to do? How could I apply this word?

I remembered that nuns took vows of celibacy. This resonated with me and I thought, 'I will marry the Lord!' I know this sounds weird but I couldn't deny the peace I was receiving as this plan was unfolding in my mind.

Those who know me will tell you I never let grass grow under my feet, so off to town to buy a wedding ring! I'm not sure what the jeweller thought when I sat in his shop with a velvet cloth placed on the table in front of me as he showed me the rings, with no-one visibly beside me! I chose a simple gold band and I was to collect it in a few days when it was made to fit me.

I went home feeling very wobbly. What if this was all in my imagination, would this be blasphemy? I knew Ron was in heaven with Him, but I still felt married to him. The Lord knew I was struggling and He said to me, 'What was Ron's greatest attribute?' Without hesitation, I replied, 'his kindness', and straight away He led me to the passage from Isaiah 54 that I'd read days before. My eyes fell upon verse 8:

'...but with everlasting kindness I will have compassion on you,' says the Lord your Redeemer.

I now knew with all my being that He had orchestrated the whole thing. I was to marry the Lord and it was settled. How was I to tell my dear friend Caren and my stepson Mark? To my absolute shock, they didn't bat an eyelid. I asked them if they'd be free to come to my wedding the following Tuesday sunset at Loughor estuary. I have no idea why they didn't question me, but they faithfully agreed to witness this vow-making ceremony of marrying the Lord.

Tuesday evening arrived, the frequent Welsh rain did not appear and the sunset was magnificent. I wore white and carried my favourite white daises. This was a deeply meaningful act of commitment for me - a Holy moment. We sang the chorus:

Purify my heart
Let me be as gold and precious silver
Purify my heart
Let me be as gold, pure gold

Refiner's fire
My heart's one desire
Is to be holy
Set apart for You, Lord
I choose to be holy
Set apart for You, my Master
Ready to do Your will

Purify my heart
Cleanse me from within and make me holy
Purify my heart
Cleanse me from my sin
Deep within.

Brian Doerksen

We had communion together, then the beautiful hymn written by Frances Ridley Havergal I spoke out as a commitment prayer to the Lord:

Take my life and let it be
Consecrated, Lord, to Thee.
Take my moments and my days,

Let them flow in endless praise.

Take my hands and let them move
At the impulse of Thy love.
Take my feet and let them be
Swift and beautiful for Thee.

Take my voice and let me sing,
Always, only for my King.
Take my lips and let them be
Filled with messages from Thee.

Take my silver and my gold,
Not a mite would I withhold.
Take my intellect and use
Every pow'r as Thou shalt choose.

Take my will and make it Thine,
It shall be no longer mine.
Take my heart, it is Thine own,
It shall be Thy royal throne.

Take my love, my Lord, I pour
At Thy feet its treasure store.
Take myself and I will be
Ever, only, all for Thee.

Frances Ridley Havergal 1874

I slipped the gold band on my ring finger and the ceremony was complete. The magnificent orange sky silhouetted the incoming tide as we walked back to the car and the sense of joy engulfed me.

I vowed to the Lord that for the rest of my life on this earth, I would be His alone. The strangest thing was that the lopsided feeling that I had experienced since Ron had died had disappeared! I was no longer single and felt totally complete.

My stepson Mark had written me a wedding card with these beautiful words on it:

To Sue - Mama Sue. May God richly bless you in the life that you've wholly abandoned to Him, a life consecrated only to Him. And in this life held firmly within His grasp, may you reflect His glory and beauty - this treasure in jars of clay. The fragrance of Jesus be poured out for many through you - a life spent for Him.

I have loved you with an everlasting love; I have drawn you with loving- kindness *(Jeremiah 31:3)*

With much love, Your God-given Son, Mark xx

How beautiful to receive these words from him. Also, the wonderful confirmation that it wasn't a fanciful thought or whim of mine to take this somewhat extreme and maybe presumptuous step. The confirmation of the Scripture verse he had given me sealed this beautiful and most precious time in my life.

The date was August 12th, 2003. How providential that years before it was the exact date of asking Jesus into my heart - August, 12th, 1982.

Isn't He so awesome!

23

PAM'S STORY

TO GIVE AND NOT TO COUNT THE COST

Before I share Pam's story with you, there is a prayer that from my youth has always stayed with me. The reason I feel it is appropriate is because it epitomises the life of dear Pam.

The prayer of generosity - to give and not to count the cost

(By Saint Ignatius of Loyola -1449-1556)

Teach us, good Lord,
to serve You as You deserve,
to give and not to count the cost,
to fight and not to heed the wounds,
to toil and not to seek for rest,
to labour and not to ask for any reward,
save that of knowing that we do Your will.
Amen

In a previous chapter, I touched on how Pam had come into our lives with such generosity towards us. Our friendship flourished and we bonded like close brother and sisters. Pam had come from a broken marriage, but her life changed when she came to faith. After meeting her at our home in Trebanos, she invited us to stay in her lovely home in a leafy district called Burghfield Common in Reading.

Pam's heart was for those less fortunate than herself. On many occasions her garage was stacked high with furniture that was surplus to her friends' needs. This was ready for the next person whose circumstances were without. What a joy it was for her to be able to be used in this way.

Her younger sister, Barbs, struggled with ill-health all her life and had developed a condition called lupus. Her struggle with this disease brought Pam to a place of sacrificial giving of her life and time as she sold her own home to move in and look after her sister. At first this was an ideal solution as Pam helped Barbs to maintain a certain degree of independence with oversight. As the disease worsened and because of Pam's health issues, they felt the only way forward was to consider full-time residential care.

The request came from Pam for me to draw on a local map a circumference of an approximate fifteen- to twenty-minute walk away from our home in Gorseinon. I did this and sent her details of suitable houses near our home. She fell in love with a compact, modern, terraced house in immaculate condition under ten minutes' walk from our home.

I was able to help with the practicalities of buying a house. Pam had agreed the sale after seeing the specifications and photographs we sent her; she came to view it and simply signed the contract and paid for it. The house was hers! Now that's what I call decisive!

On returning to Reading, Pam found a suitable residential nursing home near her new home in Gorseinon for Barbs to move into. Arrangements were made for her furniture to be collected from storage in Reading. The moving date arrived and her furniture was on the way, but Barbs was in Oxford in hospital, so Pam couldn't come.

We decided I would take delivery of her possessions, unpack and make her home ready for her new home-coming. For eighteen months this little house became a haven for Pam. Her health started to improve enough to consider having Barbs home to look after again. This little house wouldn't have been big enough. Pam is a very prayerful lady and felt this was definitely the way.

Her current house went on the market and she was able to sell it to a young Christian lady from the village at a price she could afford to pay. I'm sure Pam could have got a lot more money for her little house, but her generous spirit wanted to bless this young lady.

A deal was done and Pam found a bigger house at the other end of the village. It was a detached house on a modern housing estate. It would be ideal for Barbs, with an en-suite bedroom that would be ideal for her.

Pam secured the sale and soon moved with her sister. They were so happy being back together again. It wasn't easy. Some days were a struggle for them both with their health issues, but they worked through and made some very happy memories there.

A few years later Pam noticed a house for sale three doors from their home. During the following days she kept thinking about the house for sale, so she prayed about it and felt God spoke to her saying, 'Buy it!' So she did! All she knew was God said, 'Buy it!' He knew what His purpose was and that was good enough for her.

It was a lovely modern, detached three-bedroomed house, with one en-suite bedroom. It was light and airy and for the first two years was rented out.

We often shared, when appropriate, what we were praying for. This particular time I was praying for a young girl called Debbie whom I'd known for some years and who was completing a year at Teen Challenge. This is a Christian-based organisation that helps teenagers and adults get free from substance abuse and life-controlling problems and addictions. Debbie had been snatched from the grips of death on several occasions.

We were so proud of her as she had stuck to the strict regime of the programme. Just before the completion of the course, she had 'flu and continued to feel quite unwell and exhausted. Because of this she needed to leave, but had nowhere to live. It wasn't practical for Debbie to live with me as I was so tied up with Dad's needs and with my other commitments that it wouldn't have worked.

I asked Pam to pray about Debbie's situation as it was so heavy on my heart. Straightaway she responded and said, 'Debbie can have my house.' I didn't know that her tenants were moving out; I was astounded. When I told Debbie, she cried with relief and couldn't believe that God had done such an amazing thing for her and was so very grateful to Pam for her generosity. Pam charged only what Debbie could pay so she was never out of pocket. Debbie lived there for three years until she moved on to a flat nearer her family.

To this day Pam is still there for Debbie. Her understanding of sickness has helped her to give empathy and compassion to Debbie and so many.

During the time Debbie was living in one of Pam's houses, the Lord spoke again to Pam to buy yet another house! I knew nothing of this but shared about another young girl that a friend June had asked us to pray for, who was pregnant and 'sofa surfing' and desperate for accommodation. June was so burdened for this lovely lady and in faith had asked us to pray that at Christmas she would be able to offer her accommodation before January 1st. So that's what we did!

Can you imagine my shock when Pam calmly said she had bought another house and the lady could have it!

I remember the excitement I felt when I contacted June to say we had a beautiful house for her young lady, at a price she could afford. We were squealing with delight. The date...just before January 1st...God's timing is perfect. The pregnant young lady was over the moon with her new accommodation and happily lived there with her son for some years, finding the love and kindness of Jesus through Pam drawing her to come to know Him for herself.

Pam's desire in wanting only to do God's will is an example to us all. But there was more to follow...

Time moved on and Pam got increasingly exhausted as Barbs' health deteriorated even further. Pam felt that if she had to put Barbs into residential care again, then maybe she could find somewhere where they could go in together and share in helping her, but also have help for herself.

She found such a place and they had two rooms together - a bedroom for them both and a sitting room. Their meals and caring would be done by the staff. This seemed the right way forward. Debbie was now ready to move on to her own flat nearer her family.

Pam helped the other lady to find some good accommodation for her next home, providing the deposit to help her. The three properties were sold over the following months and for the next two years they lived together, overseen by the nursing home at Pontardulais. Pam was strengthened during this time, having the support which helped her tremendously. But they missed having that privacy that your own home brought.

A mutual friend, called Val, sadly lost her husband after a long battle with cancer. I happened to tell Pam that she was selling her home to move nearer her sons. Evidently God had been prompting Pam about a move from the nursing home and she seemed very interested, asking me more about Val's house. Before I knew it, Pam was looking to buy it! The semi-detached dormer bungalow was at the edge of an estate in an elevated position with spectacular views of Gower in the distance. This was so right for Val to have a hassle-free transaction. Contracts were signed and the house was Pam's! There were some alterations to be done, and work began.

During this time, Heddwyn and Lydiah, close friends of mine and part of Parklands Church, were looking to relocate from Nairobi. They had sold up from Swansea a decade before to pioneer a work amongst the street children of Nairobi, ploughing all their money into the project called TUMAINI KWA WATOTO - Children of Hope.

Giving up everything and living by faith without regular wages was quite a challenge, but God had met them and their growing team as they rescued children off the streets, housed them in families, paid for their education as they endeavoured to find their families and reunited them wherever possible. The team were trained to a high standard and it was the right time for them to move back to Wales to support Heddwyn's elderly mother, children and grandchildren, but they had few belongings and nowhere to live. Their trust and faith in a God who would provide for them was bringing them a total peace as they prepared to leave Africa.

We were all praying for provision for them. They had given up all for the work the Lord had called them into. We knew He wouldn't let them down but didn't expect the answer to come in the way it did.

I asked Pam to pray for them. Before I could finish telling her their situation, she said they could have the house she had just bought from Val! She insisted that God would take care of her and Barbs. Pam reminded me that the house was completely empty and would need furnishing from top to bottom. I laughed, as I have always loved this sort of challenge ever since I was in the same position. I put out a notice in the church and to friends on social media. The response was wonderful and we arranged just days before their return to have all the furniture delivered.

What fun that day was when everything arrived. We had a willing team on hand to put up beds, arrange sofas, wardrobes, and kit a complete kitchen. The only difficulty we had at the time was getting the larger furniture into the dormer bedroom. Den, one of our team, ever optimistic, decided he could take out the dormer window and haul the furniture in with a rope - no problem at all! I loved his determination.

What a lovely feeling of contentment when we opened the door for our tired but happy couple from Africa. The table was laden with food, the happiness was tangible and we were all thanking God once again for His amazing provision and the way He had led Pam once again to be His love in action.

Betty lived next door to what was now Lydiah and Heddwyn's home. She was a lovely lady and had been recently widowed. I remember thinking Pam was mad when she said that she would like to buy Betty's house if ever she moved. But God was obviously preparing her heart. Six months later Betty decided to move and Pam bought it for Barbs and herself to finally move into.

This happened very quickly and the sisters once again had privacy in a lovely home with the same spectacular views over Gower that their neighbours Heddwyn and Lydiah had. In many aspects it was a very challenging time for both of them. Barbs became more frail with added complications with her disease. She became virtually bed-bound. They had some help with daily chores but Pam stoically continued to love and care for her sister without any regard for herself.

After about a year Barbs could no longer be looked after at home as she had a stroke and needed 24/7 care. Reluctantly they both knew that it was time for Barbs to finally go permanently into a nursing home. It was such a hard decision, but Barbs was very gracious and knew that her loving, ever-caring sister could no longer look after her at home and she went into a nursing home that was convenient for Pam to visit daily. They spent long periods together and on good days they would laugh together - precious times for them.

Pam felt quite lonely in the house on her own over the months without Barbs living with her anymore and sought the Lord as to what was next.

One evening I shared my prayer request with her. We had a family of asylum seekers from Pakistan come to our church as they lived nearby. Mum, dad and three lovely young children - two girls and a boy. The youngest children were twins. They lived in a temporary home supplied by the government. They fled Pakistan for their lives and were fearful and traumatised as they began to live in a different land with a different culture.

A group of us from the church attended their court case application hearing to stay in the country. The atmosphere was tense as every word spoken was considered by the judge. We were all praying silently at the back of the court. The lawyers and barrister gave nothing away…then it was all over. We came out of court and were told he would hear the decision in three weeks. We were all so delighted that they were granted asylum, but it was short-lived and it had to go back to court again. There was so much prayer for them, and to their and our relief they decided to stay with their first decision and the family could remain in the UK.

We learnt a lot in our involvement with this dear family. They weren't allowed to earn any money until they were granted asylum. They knew many were turned back to their lands, but they knew they couldn't go back as it would have been life-threatening for them.

The moment they were granted asylum they were given notice to leave their temporary home. They tried so hard to find alternative accommodation but landlords were suspicious as the husband had no job and couldn't pay a bond as he hadn't been allowed to earn. They were desperate and their health was being affected. We were praying like mad for them as a church and this is what I was sharing with Pam.

Probably what followed next was the biggest shock Pam had ever given me. As soon as I had shared their plight with her, she immediately said to me, 'They can have my house.' I reasoned with her that maybe she needed to think it through; after all, where was she going to go? 'God will sort that out,' she said with a quiet yet confident reply, and was adamant. Within four days she had moved out, leaving the family the use of the house as she had left it, fully equipped and furnished, and charging only the rent that they would receive in benefits until he found a job.

There are no words to describe the faces of this little family. They were offered a home, beautifully furnished and with a large garden for the children to play in and with delightful panoramic views. This was a place where they could heal after the trauma of the last months. They were in awe of God's love and generosity to them. They moved in and began a new life. The children settled in a new school and jobs were soon taken.

This lovely Pakistani family 'adopted' Pam as their English mum. She is honoured by all their family and as was said at one of their family gatherings when we were present, she had made their dreams come true. This was true, sacrificial giving.

Pam was invited by Val to live temporarily with her while she decided on the next step in her life. After some weeks she found a very small bungalow to rent not too far from the nursing home. Her afternoons and part of the evenings were taken up with visits to her dear sister, who sadly got weaker and weaker. Mercifully and peacefully the Lord took her home where she would no longer have pain or suffering.

I expect you are wondering what happens next. Well, God wanted Pam to have a house again for herself and led her to a lovely compact terraced Georgian house quite near her very first home in Gorseinon. It was in a convenient area so that she could get to the shops and everything else she may need. Was this her forever home? Some years later Pam decided she would relocate to Sketty and found a delightful retirement complex and has happily settled there, still reaching out to those in need and sharing the gospel with everyone who comes into her daily path. What an example of Jesus in skin. I cannot thank God enough for bringing Pam into my life.

24

THE MOVE

He brought me out into a spacious place; he rescued me because he delighted in me (Psalm 18:19, NIV).

Life jogged on. I was always busy and that's how I liked it. We are all very different and my way of coping with loss is to be active and fulfilled in that. We all need time to grieve and some days I needed to do just that. I was aware I could get in a 'POM' (poor old me) syndrome and that wasn't good, so my various activities soon pulled me out of it.

I had started staying over at Nicholaston House so that I could co-ordinate the volunteers and spend time with my friend Helena. I would leave my home on a Sunday for church and make my way to Nicholaston in the afternoon. I would stay there until early morning on Tuesday and travel back to Dad's house and stay over a few days to support him with his needs, then manage a few days at my own home in Gorseinon, fitting in my various commitments. When I think about in now, I don't know how I managed to keep up the pace.

I greeted a new year feeling quite unwell, so I visited my doctor thinking I had some horrible disease. I was relieved to know that there was nothing physically wrong with me, but that I was simply exhausted and seriously needed to change my lifestyle, and so reluctantly I had to agree.

I spent time praying about what I should do. Common sense was saying I could no longer juggle three homes and I knew Dad's needs were going to become greater as time moved on: we actually needed to be living together. Would I move him to my house or should I sell up and move into his home - the home I had lived in all my younger years? I decided it was best for me to move to his home.

I knew deep down that he would be unhappy cooped up in a property with no outlook from the main rooms. His home had the wonderful views and a lovely garden. The decision was made and I felt His peace, so I put my house on the market. Within seventy-two hours the house was sold subject to contract.

The Lord knew this wasn't going to be easy for me to let my beloved Shalom3 go. There were so many memories Ron and I had made in the short time we had lived there. Our home was full of furniture we had collected and we had renovated much of it ourselves from items that were destined for the recycling tip. We had loved upcycling from what would have been thrown away.

Dad's home was well furnished and there was little room for more than a few personal possessions. God had all this in hand. The prospective buyer had no furniture at all and was not in a position to buy very much after he had purchased my house. I had this wonderful idea! Why didn't I offer him the house fully furnished, including all the white goods and fully equipped kitchen? He was absolutely thrilled, especially when I added that I wanted him to have them free.

I had the greatest of joy as I prepared the house for him. I placed new towels hotel-style at the base of the freshly made beds. The furniture was polished and it was spick and span. The last thing I did - and for me the most important - I left him a copy of the Bible on the dining room table with a new home card.

Dad was delighted that I was moving in with him. I explained that I would still be keeping my volunteer commitments for as long as he was well enough to be left. He agreed wholeheartedly with the plans we made to begin our new life together.

In a strange way this helped me to be able to leave Shalom3 without too much grief. Even in the five years that I had been living on my own, I had become quite independent. Little did I know what was in store for me, but I knew that whatever was ahead God had promised to be in it with me. I had no idea that this chapter in my life would take me to the very edge.

It started well, at least for the first few weeks. My personal possessions were moved in and of course my nana's treasured sewing machine table that had become my desk. My bedroom was the upstairs guest room. A light and airy room with views over the distant mountains and Kilvey Hill, as well as a view of Swansea Bay. I had my own phone line put in to save any hassle as I knew Dad would have a problem with my usage. I had moved him into a downstairs room some months previously for safety reasons as he was having difficulty with the stairs.

I'm sure it must have been strange for him having me living with him. Although he was having his needs met by me, he had great difficulty in accepting that I was still maintaining my volunteer commitments even though he had agreed in theory when we had talked through the conditions of my living there. I expect he was wanting me to replicate the role that he had with Mum. He was used to having full attention and began to complain and grumble at the time I spent away from the house. Bit by bit I had to give up areas of my volunteer work, but held on tightly to my ward visiting that I loved so much.

My sister Hilary would take charge when I had a break. I found this old list that I had made with strict instructions to follow while I was away!

HILARY - Dad's needs. You may find this useful. Please can you:

- Phone him twice a day when you are not seeing him.
- Wash his hair twice a week.
- Wash his feet once a week (he'll tell you what is needed).
- Washing once a week, if it's raining use the dryer.
- Clean pyjamas/undies/socks, etc. airing or in cupboard by his bed.
- Spare towels/bedding in the fitted cupboard in my room.
- Should be no need to change bed as I will do it, but there is a spare set in the downstairs airing cupboard.
- Library books may need changing, opening times in the bag with books.
- Tablets will be sorted, but you will need to put one up for him from the supplies ready sorted.
- Shopping as usual, please can you top up his ready-made meals, but no curry and rice 'cos he's off it!

- Please can you pick up a TV programme guide for the second week I'm away.
- Please can you water the plants a few times a week.
- Upstairs will be fine, but please could you put some loo stuff to freshen up.
- Please could you hoover floors downstairs and give a quick dust just once a week.
- If the lifeline is pressed, they will talk and will cancel from their end if it's a false alarm. It's linked to the telephone, so if his phone isn't working you will need to let BT know as he is on high priority.
- It will help him feel confident if you keep him reassured. He finds it hard when he doesn't know what's going to happen.
- I'm sure you will manage fine. Have a lovely time with him.

25

CHILDREN OF HOPE, KENYA
God sets the lonely in families

I was approaching my sixtieth year and had made some special plans for 2007. I had always wanted to go up in a hot-air balloon. We also had a trip planned with the church to go away for two weeks on mission to Nairobi to our friends of TKW (Children of Hope), the Christian charity headed up by Heddwyn and Lydiah Williams from Wales, who rescued children off the streets.

Let me share my experience as I recall from writings at the time:

Trip to Kenya - August 2007

My time in Trinidad in 2001 prepared me in part for my visit to Kenya - the sheer volume of people, chaotic traffic, noise, wild driving, chaos, which I'm sure to the Kenyans are the normal way of life. A sea of black faces looking onto our team of white faces. Strong unfamiliar smells, mostly unpleasant making the tummy turn over. So many people on foot, walking in droves to the next port of call, to a bus stop, or to a tree in shade to stretch out and sleep under.

In the city I was mesmerised with the mix of rich, poor and very poor. There was a sense of urgency in many, to continue on their journey to the next shop, appointment or meeting; others, less fortunate souls, wandering around aimlessly looking for something to do, maybe something to eat. There was a sense of covering your steps to make sure you were safe from opportunists who see white westerners as all rich and potentially good to pick-pocket from.

The traffic and driving were something from hell! There seemed to be no road sense and no code of respect - cars, buses, etc. all overtook inside and outside - it was free for all, and relied on hope that you got to your destination in one piece, which we did, by the travelling mercies of God.

It's worth mentioning that I read an article in the local paper that said many tourists are being put off coming to Kenya because of the atrocious conditions on the roads! I can only say they are a nightmare. There was a marked difference as we journeyed away from the hubbub of city life, with its barrenness and bleak sights, and into the country; although since a change in government, there has been a marked change in the parks and streets for the better.

The scenery changes to the beauty of lush greenery in the form of banana trees, maize, etc. growing on the side of the road, and the hills with allotments full of fruit and vegetables of all sorts. Many of the people were in traditional dress, as they came to try to sell their wares to us. This was so refreshing from those in the city. This was Africa.

As we journeyed through to our destinations, we passed many villages - some just small huts in the middle of the trees. It didn't take much imagination to go back in time and see them in your mind's eye, in mud huts and tribal dress. There was a smell of smoke as so many were cooking on outdoor fires. I was aware that they would do anything to try to make money for food, and they worked hard just to survive. At each street corner there seemed to be a person who had set up a fire and was cooking corn to sell. They always seemed to have hungry customers who threw their eaten remains down on the floor to add to the other rubbish littering the ground. When the light faded, despite no pavements, only hard-packed, unlit, mud sidewalks, so many people bustled about, continuing with their chores - it was a world apart from ours in the West.

Joseph Kangethe Hall is a detention centre run by the Kenyan government. It is used to house children who have been found living on the streets, arresting them, detaining them and bringing them to a safe place. These children could be from seven years old upwards. Some have been orphaned. Many parents die of AIDS. Some children living in extreme poverty try the city for the hope of a better life. Some are thrown out of their homes and have no choice but to live on the streets.

I must admit to feeling very apprehensive on the journey there. We had an overall picture of what we could expect, but I was not prepared to take in the reality of how these kids lived. We drove into the complex. People seemed to be scattered around the perimeter of the hall; it felt sad, dry and barren, but all so necessary to keep the kids from the streets.

There were a few children at the entrance, shabbily dressed and all very inquisitive at our team of white faces. We went into the hall and my first impression was a sea of black faces wondering what we had come for. Had we brought some hope to them. For me the smell in there and the sight of the dorms, walls and floors made my stomach turn over, especially as it got hot in there with hardly any windows. I had to concentrate on not being sick.

The idea was that we would work together with the Kenyan team, playing action games and getting to know the kids. First of all, we introduced ourselves and I felt so moved that when the kids were asked alongside many of the others in the team, a very small lad remembered my name; his name was Mike 'Tyson' and I took him into my heart. He had such a sad face and at the start didn't want to join in, so he helped us and we were so encouraged that by the end of the morning he was smiling and happy.

It was an amazing experience to work with the Kenya team who were so full of energy and fun. We met some of the officials who ran the place and they were so very grateful of the contact we had there. When we gave out half-a-loaf of bread each and endless mugs of Kenyan tea, Mike Tyson was amazing as he was sharing his ration with his friend. It was so moving.

Mike 'Tyson'

Yes, this little sad-looking boy, who looked no older than seven, great emptiness and pain behind his eyes, just melted my heart. I had made a friend. I gave him the 'job' of looking after the whistle to control the games we were going to play and his little face lit up, and we led the game together, hand in hand…what a special time. I learnt after that Mike had been desperate to be reunited with his family, but however hard the team tried to find a lead for his family, it never came to anything. He didn't want a foster family, but his real family. As a treat for the boys, we gave out half-a-loaf of bread each and endless mugs of Kenyan tea. I watched them all devour it as if they'd been given a banquet. Mike Tyson took his ration and began sharing...I was moved to tears...he was now firmly locked in my heart...oh, I prayed for him.

Just two months later we heard this story from the team. They had continued trying to find Mike's family. Two years had elapsed since he had seen them; he'd left when his mother's new partner had not got on with him and he made his way begging and living on the streets of Nairobi until he was caught and put into detention. Sometimes they would take him with them when they visited other areas outside Nairobi to see if he could remember any landmarks (believe me, they are few and far between).

On October, 17th, 2007, Mike had got up, prayed and prayed, and told the team that this would be the day that he would find his mother!

He gave away everything he owned; scruffy clothing is all he had - his only possessions the clothes he stood in. Then began a long journey towards Naivasha as he felt he might live near there. God was with him and was doing the most incredible thing. Grace, who was leading the team that day, borrowed a camera from an onlooker and took the actual pictures as the story unfolded. This was the miracle that Mike had prayed for. After two years they walked into his village and here was his mum. God had answered his prayers. What a wonderful outcome for these faithful TKW workers!

The Swansea team began building relationships with some of the children. We saw Grace and some of the

Kenyan team at work, as they interacted with some kids that they had been helping.

The reality was that these kids were being looked after as well as those employed to help them, yet it fell so short of the standards that we would consider basic. Our first thoughts were, if only we could throw away the dirty beds and bedding, clean and paint the walls and floors, making it a better environment for them to live in. But we learnt to understand that if we, or others, did that it would be a place that they wouldn't want to leave. This way, although they knew they would receive regular food however meagre, it was not an ideal environment to be a permanent home. This is hard for us from the West to understand, but it made great sense, and we trusted our African brothers and sisters to know best.

It was Chris Jones' birthday and the Kenyan team bought a cake, so we sang in English, Swahili and Welsh, which was wonderful. Chris then cut the two cakes and gave each person a piece; the kids loved it too. I had the privilege of praying for them all, and we were so moved at the prayers some of the children made to the Lord - an incredible experience.

I went back only to say goodbye, whereas some of the team had spent a part of each day working, teaching, playing and praying with the guys there. It was so obvious that the Swansea team had made wonderful links and bonding with many of the individuals, and as we left, many tears were shed both by the females and the males of our group.

It was a place I will never forget and I know for many of these children that this is the start of their journey to a future and a hope as the Kenya Children of Hope team are led to those who are receptive for their help. They will then try to unite them with their parents or relatives, or maybe find a foster mum and a family to love them.

Every Child Needs a Family

Three weeks later we heard this news. Praise God from the rooftops as we have just heard that Mike Tyson miraculously, through prayer and the huge efforts of the team at TKW, had found his family and was united with them again.

Kiberra is an infamous slum area in Nairobi that houses over one million people. It has been described as 'hell on earth'. I was very apprehensive when it was our time to visit Kiberra because other members of our team had gone in and were physically shaken at what they had seen and said the smells were like nothing they had ever experienced. In fact, they found that their clothes smelt of what can only be Kiberra and felt compelled to completely change their clothes on their return.

However much you have been prepared, nothing can be reality unless you experience the sights for yourself. We pensively approached Kiberra. It was within easy walking distance from TKW offices. The sheer volume of people couldn't help but cause you to wonder how people could live under these conditions.

As we approached, we were greeted with rows of stalls selling charcoal for their fires for cooking. Many children were shoeless, darting in and out of the customers, the sellers and all that was going on. The noise, heat and smells caught at the back of your throat.

The packed, flattened mud walkways were edged with open sewerage gutters running through, filled with rubbish and dogs, searching for scraps of food. Many of the slums had shop fronts selling anything from jewellery to cooked intestines! Yet amongst these slums there were many 'churches', little huts with roughly-painted graffiti, but saying 'Jesus is Lord'. Jesus was in these slums and with these people.

The walkways were uneven, slippery and quite dangerous as you were aware that you had to keep looking down for fear of what you would tread on. Children played happily in these small pathways, unaware that they were classed as one of the poorest areas in Africa, maybe in the third world. Wherever we went because we were white you would hear, 'How are you?' in their lovely African accent, white teeth shining at you complete with a big smile as you spoke back to them with an English/Swahili reply.

As we walked a little deeper into Kiberra, the smell increased as well as the feeling of being unsafe. We knew it was time to turn back as we had seen enough to last us a lifetime. I'm glad we were able to visit Kiberra, so that I will always remember how fortunate I am, blessed to have all I have as I live in the West.

As we ploughed our way back through the crowds, we quickly came back to the open road and fresh air.

We left Kiberra, but the sights we saw will never leave us.

Karatina and Nairobi

One of the highlights of my trip to Kenya was when I was able to meet Joseph Thiongo in person and his dear foster mum, Mary. Mary had been quite unwell for some time and was receiving blood in the local hospital. It was lovely of Grace to take us to meet her.

Karatina is a beautiful place. Lydiah Williams and her family come from these parts. It is full of lush green vegetation: tea plantations, coffee beans, maize, bananas, etc. - such a change from the aridness of the city and districts of Nairobi. The climate was cooler and more moist than the city of Nairobi which made it an ideal place for the various plantations. The culture was far more traditionally old Africa. English wasn't spoken much by the older generation and dress was far more traditional. The air was clean and wonderful, which was so different from the diesel and petrol-laced air of Nairobi.

To meet Joseph Thiongo was such a thrill. Grace, Chris and I were welcomed by him and he showed us the tea plantation and the area around their home. They were beautiful surroundings. The house that was built in 1971 was in such need of rebuilding (this was being done by Team 2 in the following weeks). Joseph was nervous meeting us, but was delighted to show us around. We were introduced to the milking cow that Bri and Harriet had given them in 2006. Margaret, Mary's sister, made us Kenyan tea and a Kenyan meal. Grace tucked into it heartily, as well as Chris, but I just ate a few morsels so as not to offend!

After that we walked around the area and then waited for the truck to come that was bringing some of the building materials ahead of Team 2, so that all would be ready for them when they came to rebuild Mary's house for her.

Oh, the joy to know that Mary would be able to have a better home, with a roof that was not threatening to fall in, with no light shining through the wood joints, and keeping the colder air out and warm air in. It was so little to ask.

I was so thrilled that the Lord had made provision for Mary and Joseph to have a new home which would help make life so much easier, and hopefully Mary's health would improve. We prayed that the time Team 2 had in rebuilding the house would be a special time as they got to know Mary, Margaret, her sister, Joseph Thiongo and the community there.

I wanted to support the family by employing a tea-picker. When Mary was well, she was able to pick the tea from her small tea plantation; this would be sold and would provide money for food and other necessities. I hoped too that as I shared with more people, we might be able to secure Joseph's education in some way and take some pressure from them. Mary had chosen to give Joseph a home, and had known many difficulties with her health for some years.

We were saddened to hear many years later that Mary had died. Joseph Thiongo's life unfortunately turned for the worst as he got in with the wrong crowd and eventually lost his life. Life is very fragile. We live in hope that in part we can make a difference.

June, Chris and I were taken on a city walk with Grace and Frank as guides. Our first stop was at Central Park. This appeared to be a beautiful tranquil park just before you got to the hustle and bustle of the city. As we reflected on the peaceful scene, Grace explained that just five years before each tree would have been a home for a street child. They would live, sleep, cook under each tree, sniff glue and other drugs or use alcohol in an attempt to dull and block out the pain of a hopeless life. It was hard to imagine two such different scenarios.

Since the new government has come in, it has been working at improving conditions in the city. If the street children were caught, they would be arrested and taken to a detention centre. Grace explained that it was very rare to find children on the streets now as they hid from the authorities. The Tumaini Kwa Watoto Team hadn't seen them for some months.

As we were shown around the places that were so significant and many trees where the street children had lived, Frank told us his story. He had once been a glue sniffer and a street kid himself.

At the age of sixteen he was approached by some people telling him if he went with them, they would give him a better life. He believed them and was taken to Uganda. There he was trained to fight and become a soldier. His initiation was to kill a person, drink some of the blood, cut out the tongue, cook it, then eat it; this he had to do.

We were horrified and wondered how anyone could get over such an atrocity. He said that after a time he could take it no longer and decided to try to escape. He saw his chance when a juggernaut came near him; he got between the wheels on the undercarriage, hanging on for 48 hours until he could hang on no longer. He thought he would have to let go knowing the back wheels would run over him and he would be killed, but as he let go an amazing thing happened. The lorry stopped and despite having injured his back on the fall to the ground, he was able to escape and was back in Kenya.

God was with him and despite an up-and-down journey, he eventually found himself as a volunteer with Tumani Kwa Watoto working with street kids, just like he was. May God bless him and use him mightily in this work.

We walked further into the city, taking in the sights and stories on the way. When we got to the site of where the famous Masai Market is held, Grace, with her ever keen and discerning sight, spotted a group of children under a tree across from the busy roundabout heaving with traffic. She was amazed as the team had not seen any street children in the open on the streets of Nairobi for months. We began to make our way across the busy road but as we did we noticed the little group disappearing.

As we began walking on the grassy verge towards the tree, out of the blue came two young children. Grace and Frank began talking to them in Swahili. We looked at the younger lad, his clothes torn and a hidden bottle containing glue was shoved out of our view as he talked to Grace. You couldn't help but notice his teeth; so many Africans, despite their often-poor diet, still have beautiful white teeth. But this young lad didn't. You could see that by hanging the bottle in his mouth, held by his teeth to sniff glue, the damage was done and so obvious.

Grace with her usual lovely manner, talked, understanding what was happening in this young life. She had met him before. Frank too talked and warmed the heart of the lad he spoke to. After they had talked, we all prayed for and with them, and they went on their way.

We began to walk and under another tree was a young couple with a baby. They looked so shabby and ill. We were taken aback, Grace talked to them, and we parted feeling quite helpless.

Amazingly, as we continued to walk over to the tree, we saw the gang of street children from across the road. They began to appear one by one until they were all there talking and listening to Grace, and we sang and prayed together. What an awesome experience!

We marvelled that God had especially ordained that we would meet, talk, sing and pray with these lads. We were beginning to understand the enormous task the Tumaini Kwa Watoto had in their mission to bring a future and a hope to these broken youngsters.

As we finished our time, we continued to walk on and I managed to get a picture of them under the tree where we had met them. This has been so etched in my memory and my heart. I thank God for the hearts of Heddwyn and Lydiah and their devoted team, who have given their lives sacrificially for such as these kids.

Whatever you did for one of the least of these brothers of mine, you did for me (Matthew 25:40).

It was a joy to visit the New Life Home, which is a Christian charity that takes in abandoned babies; some are left in toilets, on the streets, etc. The work has grown over the years. The building reflects the lovely conditions the babies live in until they are adopted. The standard of care and hygiene is second to none.

There was a relaxed, happy atmosphere and the babies and toddlers played in various crèche rooms with the help of the staff and many volunteers who play a big part in the care programme. There are children's Christian songs playing quietly in the background and an air of calm and a tranquil relaxed environment. Obviously, the children and all involved in this wonderful work were bathed in the presence of God. I loved it there.

We marvelled at the living conditions at the New Life Home. For these babies whose start in life had been the worst one could ever have, it was wonderful to know that they will soon be adopted, cherished and loved. I thank God for this place.

June had given us a fright only two days after our arrival: she ended up having emergency treatment. As we waited for test results at Nairobi Private Hospital, we feared DVT, but we breathed out when the diagnosis was phlebitis. It was worth every penny it cost! What a relief! We made our way back to Heddwyn and Lydiah's home and ended up having supper at midnight!

Beacon of Hope is a Christian charity that has a heart for adults who need to have an HIV test and counsels them if they find they have HIV/AIDS. The tests are free for them. They then help those who have a positive result, teaching the women new skills, helping them with the children who also might have HIV or AIDS. They have many volunteers to help with this work and make many crafts to sell to help run the place.

There was a lovely warmth and acceptance as all who come for help are treated sensitively and without judgement. The day we visited was full of children enjoying a holiday bible club. The conditions were as good as they could give with the provisions they have. It was filled with love and service to the Lord.

When we arrived, we were met by a lovely lady who had the position of counsellor. She was so gentle and took time to explain all about the work they did. She loved the Lord and was thrilled when Grace asked if we could pray for her, which we did and it delighted her. She took us around the building, sharing so much with us. Like most places we had visited, the toddlers were thrilled to see us and little hands went up in the air to be picked up - so very trusting. We were so aware how different things are in the UK as we couldn't pick up someone else's child without their permission. These Africans seem to trust us so much.

***

What wonderful memories as I reflect on what I had written ten years ago. The work is still going on. More and more children are being rescued by the team each day. We thank God for these faithful souls who give tirelessly, often with little provision for themselves. Great will be their reward in eternity.

This mission trip made my sixtieth year something I would never forget and I still draw from those memories as we continue to pray for and support this wonderful team at TKW.

Returning home after this life-changing experience took some adjusting. The first weekend home was a wet, grey, miserable, colourless day. I was missing vibrant Kenya already!

26

HILARY

Around this time, I could see a change in Hilary, my sister. She just wasn't herself. I was devastated at the news that she had secondary brain tumours. Radiotherapy would be imminent.

As a hairdresser, Hilary always had immaculate hair, so as soon as she was told she would lose her hair, she ordered a very stylish wig which looked great on her. Steroids were given to keep things at bay. She improved for a time with the steroids that were prescribed, but I knew her prognosis wasn't good.

The next few months were very special for me as I was able to have some precious input into her life. I was able to support her in a small way and although the disease was robbing her of so much, she became childlike, full of fun and even joyful.

When she was hospitalised, I was able to spend many hours with her at Singleton hospital Oncology Ward 12, and because the ward I worked on as a chaplaincy visitor was opposite, I was able to slip across and do my ward visiting also.

When Hilary was discharged, we had a wonderful nursing support team called SPICE. These dedicated trained people see to the needs of patients in the community at the end of their lives and make it possible for those who want to be at home.

Hilary left us for heaven late one Spring afternoon in April 2009. She had fought bravely and because of her faith in Jesus we knew she had eternal life. This is the tribute I shared at her funeral:

'Most of you will know that I am Hilary's big sister and over the past few months I have had the great privilege to be just that for her. What a journey she has had, especially over the last twelve months. I have been so proud of her as she faced radiotherapy, lost her hair and everything that brain tumours cause, but she fought on…my brave sister…

'Thank you, Allan, Laura and Karen for letting me walk this walk over the past weeks with you. We have laughed with Hilary and cried with her, and despite all this, her personality shone through and she was dearly loved by all. Even the other patients forgave her when she woke them up one morning to tell them they were having bacon and egg for breakfast, only to find it was her wishful thinking!

'Special thanks to the staff of Ward 12, the community district nurses, the Tŷ Olwen palliative care team and the fabulous Spice Team, all who so lovingly cared for Hilary in the last few months of her life. And those fantastic friends of hers who faithfully came day after day, not knowing what to expect, but came anyway and always made Hilary laugh as she did them. Yes, even happy memories at such a difficult time for her.

'Hilary, was a committed Christian and, it's with great sadness that her time on earth has ended, BUT SHE LIVES ON! Her soul and spirit have gone to heaven, the hope of glory. She left this earth peacefully and with great dignity, knowing and believing this Scripture:

For God so loved the world, that He gave His only Son, so that everyone who believes in Him will not perish but have eternal life (John 3:16).

'I glanced in her Bible and her book called *My Dear Child* with words she had underlined in a section of her book about 'Glory' - words that God might speak to His children:

I want you to know that the cloud of My glory overshadows you. You never need to live under a cloud of oppression or darkness when you can live under the cloud of My glory. Wherever you go, that cloud goes with you. My divine glory is your inheritance.

I want you to live in the hope of glory. No matter what you experience now, glory awaits you. Jesus will come again as the Lord of glory. Beyond this life you will come into the full radiance of My glory that at present you only know partially. When you see Me face to face, you will be transformed into My likeness. This will be completion of what I have planned and My glory will be reflected perfectly in you.

'A close and dear friend wanted to convey her sympathy to me and couldn't find the words. As a singer, she found God putting the words of this old song into her mind. I close with the words of this song that I believe could be just the words Hilary might have said to bring us comfort:

When all my labours and trials are o'er
And I am safe on that beautiful shore
Just to be near the dear Lord I adore
Will through the ages be glory for me

When by the gift of His infinite grace
I am accorded in Heaven a place
Just to be there and to look on His face
Will through the ages be glory for me

Friends will be there I have loved long ago
Joy like a river around me will flow
Yet, just a smile from my Saviour I know
Will through the ages be glory for me

CHORUS

Oh that will be glory for me
Glory for me
Glory for me
Glory for me
When by His Grace I shall look in His face
That will be glory for me.'

27

HIS GRACE IS SUFFICIENT

Losing Hilary was very hard, especially for her husband, children and grandchildren. I felt a great sense of loss of my only sibling. Dad never got over losing Hilary. He had felt especially close to her. They were very similar in many ways. It is always devastating when a child passes before a parent.

Just weeks after losing Hilary, Dad had his ninetieth birthday. I knew Hilary would have wanted us to celebrate, so reluctantly he allowed us to do so. Despite our deep sadness, we made the day very special for him, with many friends popping in with cards and gifts. His heart was warmed by the love that he received and was pleased that he'd decided to let us organise it for him. Despite our deep sadness, we made more happy memories as we celebrated his landmark of ninety years.

Dad loved his football and rugby and ever since I was a child weekend sport viewing was sacrosanct. One particular weekend when he was in the middle of an exciting rugby match, I decided that I would clear his old bedroom upstairs.

The utility furniture was post-war and the room was now obsolete as his bedroom because he slept downstairs. Having managed many things on my own over the years, this task was not daunting to me. I'm a very determined lady so with the help of a sheet on the stairs I took out a double and a single wardrobe and a large dressing table, slid them down the stairs and took them out of the house by the front door and 'dismantled' them ready for collection. Fortunately for me, Dad was totally oblivious and I was able to make myself a little haven to have the much-needed space I longed for.

Over the following months I saw a marked deterioration in his health. He became quite depressed and more difficult to please. Increased visits to the hospital and doctor's surgery became his main outings. He needed help with his personal hygiene and eventually agreed to having a carer to help him. This increased as he needed more help.

I never regretted my decision to look after Dad, but I underestimated the sheer exhaustion that would often threaten to overwhelm me. His diagnosis of vascular dementia explained a lot of reasons why his behaviour was changing. It was probably the hardest thing I've ever done and I'm sure I could have done better.

Years later I had the opportunity to understand dementia a little more and how I wished I'd had this information when I was looking after Dad.

He would often fall and it would be impossible for me to lift him up. The ambulance would be called and because of the sheer volume of their calls we would often wait hours for them to arrive, leaving him lying distraught on the floor. I would make him as comfortable as I could until they arrived to lift him up and check him over.

We spent well over a thousand pounds on a special inflating cushion similar to the ones the paramedics used. It really needed two people to operate, but I would struggle on my own ending up like a contortionist with Dad precariously perched on the inflating cushion with me praying that he wouldn't fall off! He was always thankful that he was off the floor and that we didn't need to ring for an ambulance. This of course was far more traumatic for Dad and I must say I used to breathe a sigh of relief when I got him safely back into his chair or back into bed to check him over for any injuries.

I have always loved gardening and had taken on responsibility for Dad's large garden some years before. I found it very therapeutic even though it was hard work. I set about making the garden low maintenance. The hedges were cut to a manageable height. It took me many weeks but when I progressed from a hand saw to an electric one, this made life a lot easier.

The lawns took over the rose beds, and borders too got absorbed into grass areas. I had the patio area extended so that he could sit out if he wanted to and enjoy the lovely views.

The large side garden that had once been cultivated by Dad as a fruit and vegetable patch was now a bramble wilderness. Over a few seasons we had it sprayed to kill the roots then got the bulldozer in to dig it and flatten the area. It was later lawned and another area was manageable.

To the side of the house the wall was higher for more privacy and drive gates were erected. I think he was pleased, especially as I was paying for most of it.

I loved being in the fresh air and meeting the many different people who talked to me as they went through the lane at the edge of the garden to get to the local school where Dad once taught. I always made sure I was within earshot of my father so that I could also see to his needs.

I always felt close to God when I was in the garden. The sky was my ceiling, the warmth of the sun and the sound of the dawn chorus each morning accompanied the beautiful sunrise that I could see from my bedroom window.

I loved decorating and often had the paintbrush out freshening the walls with a lick of paint. One Saturday afternoon when Dad was totally absorbed in his rugby, I decided to give the walls in the lounge a lick of paint. I moved his chair near the TV and as unobtrusively as I could make myself with the paint roller in hand, I proceeded to paint the walls. By the time the match was over the walls were completed. I was relieved that his side won, which helped his reaction considerably!

I knew my future was in God's hands. I'd always said that I would move after my Dad's days probably to a little over 50s' apartment near my church in Sketty with no garden responsibilities and easy to lock up and go when I visited my family in other parts of Europe.

Dad's health continued to go downhill. His heart failure, diabetes, chronic bronchitis and macular degeneration accompanied the diagnosis of vascular dementia. I was very concerned with his mental state and he was seen by the psychiatric team who suggested to him that he went into the assessment unit for a few days as he was quite unwell and confused. He agreed and went in later that day.

I was so relieved that he would be getting professional help. It was heart-breaking seeing him there, but we knew it was the best for him. A few days later I had a phone call from the hospital to say they were very concerned and they were having him transferred to a medical ward. I spent part of each day in the ward. They had found a gall stone that was stuck outside the gall bladder and that was giving him a lot of trouble. Each time they made arrangements to try to remove it, they had to cancel as he was too ill to cope with the endoscopy procedure.

The staff were wonderful and kept me updated each day. Antibiotics were not working and his aged body was failing. I think he knew I was there and I slept beside him on an air mattress. He slept peacefully and the next morning he quietly slipped away.

It all happened so quickly. Those years of struggling were now over. He had said after Mum had died that if he could have ten more years he would be happy. He was granted twenty more years and had ninety-three years upon this earth.

28

SURVIVAL KIT FOR CARERS...
WHO CARES FOR THEM?

He reached down from on high and took hold of me; he drew me out of deep waters. He rescued me from my powerful enemy, from my foes, who were too strong for me. They confronted me in the day of my disaster, but the Lord was my support. He brought me out into a spacious place; he rescued me because he delighted in me (Psalm 18:16-19 NIV).

One of the most satisfying roles on this earth is to be able to care for someone; to let the love in your heart pour out in the most practical of ways and to know your loved one responds with appreciation and gratefulness. Is there anything more beautiful? Maybe that's what I thought when I was wearing rose-coloured glasses!

I'm sure there are many out there where this has been their experience and that's wonderfully gratifying, but I think in many cases it is the exception rather than the rule.

It is so very hard for the person needing care. They don't want to be a burden; they begin to lose their independence and hate it. Very often their anger at the situation is directed at the person who has sacrificed their lives to take on their needs of being cared for. How do we know how it would feel unless we ourselves are, or have been, in that situation?

Even by taking this into consideration, it often goes out of the window when we are taken to our limits with tiredness, stress and frustration. Often we are juggling many other plates in the air at the same time which can take us to the end of our tether.

I remember such a day in my caring role with Dad. Everything I was doing wasn't right for him; I was tired and frustrated. I didn't have much more left to give. I went upstairs to my haven room and became completely overwhelmed. I did something I had never done before and I sat in the corner of the room in a foetal position with my head tucked firmly into my arms. I had had enough.

I felt so much anger, even anger with God as I felt such a failure as a carer. I had always known His grace to be sufficient, but at that very moment it didn't seem so.

Immediately the phone rang. I wasn't going to answer it so that I could stay in my 'poor old me state'. Annoyingly it continued to ring and I knew if I left it, Dad would have been disturbed. I picked it up and a lady I didn't personally know was asking for help. I thought, oh no God, not now! Then an amazing thing happened as I listened to her needs and felt her pain; all my anger and frustrations left me. His grace is most certainly sufficient! Because I took that phone call, I had made a lovely new friend who became such a source of joy to me as we've shared our journey caring for our loved ones.

'Who cares for the carers?' became a passion for me during my various caring roles. So often, especially when caring for the elderly, they can have unreal expectations of us carers and we find there is a need to put in boundaries.

This may seem a little uncaring but very necessary for the carer not to be totally absorbed into their role. It is right for the carer to have some time and space for themselves and of course other family members who have to take a back seat. Many carers feel guilty if they want some time for themselves. It is essential to be able to give wholesome and loving care.

So, who cares for the carers? The responsibility has to start with us. We need to value ourselves and take regular time out by having respite. Arranging for our family members, friends or an organisation who will sit with our loved one to have that much deserved break or holiday is also essential.

This may be hard for the loved one to understand and may put up a protest, but we must stick to our guns and get it booked. The break will recharge our batteries and energise us so that we have renewed vigour to continue our sacrificial role.

I can never thank enough those friends who regularly visited Dad, listened to endless wartime stories with genuine interest, played Scrabble at quite a competitive level and often lost to this ex-teacher! They were supporting me through good and bad times and keeping my sanity!

You can only do your best. Sometimes that won't feel enough, but it is. We cannot rescue our loved one out of sickness, but we can support and love in the centre of it.

29

RENEWED VISION

Loss was an emotion that had become far too familiar to me. I had learnt a coping mechanism that worked for me and that was to throw myself into a project. I knew only too well that God's ways are very often not ours. I mentioned in an earlier chapter that after Dad's days I had thought to move to a purpose-built flat and go into semi-retirement mode, but He was having none of it!

As a caring person, I knew that was His gift in my nature that would never go away, but I knew that I could not be a full-time carer again. It had taken me to a very low state and I had a peace about my decision. Aunty Betty, a spinster, had other ideas!

Over the years as I cared for Dad, I also kept a close eye on her as she had multiple health issues. She had hoped that after Dad's days I would pack up and move in with her and be her full-time carer. She was very dismayed when I reluctantly told her that I couldn't do that for her. I wasn't wonder woman and realised how very weak I was at times. I know she was cross with me but I stood firm, assuring her that I would always oversee her and her affairs. It wasn't the easiest of relationships for us but we managed to maintain it for the most part.

The months after Dad's passing were taken up with all the necessary legalities such as the solicitor, will, probate, etc. When it was all completed, I proceeded to buy my share of the property I was living in as I knew His plan for me was to stay in Dad's house.

Over the months prior to Dad's passing, God was working on my heart. My desire to move away was being changed by Him. Those years at Nicholaston House and all I had learnt there were to be put to use in this very place. My home would become a cosy short-term retreat for weary ladies. The rest would unfold as it came into being. I was so excited! I knew that my inheritance would all be needed to bring this plan into being. It was scary but also wonderfully thrilling at the prospect of not now going into retirement…what was in store for me?

30

ENLARGE MY TENT

Enlarge the place of your tent, stretch your tent curtains wide, do not hold back; lengthen your cords, strengthen your stakes (Isaiah 54:2 NIV).

Although I had kept the property well maintained, I knew that there was modernising needed and I thought about having a conservatory added. I contacted Ade, a Christian builder from my church. It was so good to talk through possibilities with him.

The conservatory idea updated to a large light and airy orangery room which would be a much more usable room in all seasons. It would have large velux windows in the high sloping roof with windows and a French door to the side. Underfloor heating would complete the comfort it would bring. It would be built to maximise the panoramic views. This sounded wonderful.

We talked about various updates to the house, including a new boiler, replastering any of the old walls and putting up new ceilings in most rooms. The dining room would be knocked through to have bifolding doors opening up the rooms when needed. I was so excited and after the estimate was in, I gladly accepted it.

Work would start on the updating of the interior of the house in a couple of months at the start of the new year, followed by the building of the orangery in early summer.

I was so glad I had had the large attic floored and suitable for storage after I had moved in some years before as I was going to need to box and pack up most of my belongings to have the extensive renovations done. I am not known for being minimalistic and Ade described me as an organised hoarder! What can I say? It's because of my Blue Peter mentality of keeping things just in case I can reuse them!

Most people dread the upheaval, but for some strange reason I love being in the middle of such things. My mum used to say that when I was a child and there was an upheaval, I would say, 'Let's have an adventure!' We are all wired differently. That's not to say that occasionally I would feel overwhelmed with the chaos.

Ade and I would powwow together to organise our schedule. I would often hop on a flight to the Channel Islands to visit my daughter and have an enjoyable break while he and Jay, his apprentice, would be working hard on the renovations. It was lovely to be sent pictures by email of the progress.

I remember the time Ade was working on the lounge with new soundproofed walls and new ceilings. He was taking out the old central heating back boiler from the fireplace and came up with an idea of a log burner in its place with a beam over the fireplace. He would email me pictures so that I could approve his plans. The result was stunning and transformed the room. What a clever man!

When the foundations were being laid and just as the cement was being poured into the footings we prayed and sank four small stones from Israel into the corners of the foundation to signify that this would be a special place and kept for the purposes of God.

I took pictures from beginning to the end of the build, enjoying every minute and often getting stuck in with the guys, keeping them stocked with endless cups of tea and the occasional Welsh cakes, scones or homemade soup.

Philip Chatfield, a very talented sculptor, offered to carve me a stone plaque to put into the wall. I was delighted. I knew he had used Jersey granite when he built the chapel at Nicholaston House. He suggested that when I went to stay with my daughter, we should visit the quarry where he had purchased the stone. He gave me rough measurements of the size he needed. I found the quarry and spoke with the owner about the pink coloured Jersey stone we wanted. He explained the stone I wanted was no longer quarried in Jersey but he had a small amount in store. I gave him the measurements that Philip required and was asked to collect it in a few days.

We returned and were quite astounded at the size of the cut granite. Michael, the stone dresser who worked with the owner, heaved it into the car and belted it into the front seat as the boot wasn't able to open. It weighed twelve stones! How was I going to get this back to Wales? I began to think that perhaps this wasn't such a good idea after all.

I returned to Wales pondering how on earth I was going to get this rather large piece of granite over from Jersey. On my next visit to Jersey a few months later I decided that I would ask the men at the quarry to cut it in half so that I could then get it shipped over to Wales.

The owner asked if I could ring back after the Easter break, which I did. He said there was no need for it to be cut into two as Michael who worked with him was actually coming to Wales to visit family and had offered to bring it to me. I couldn't believe it and to be honest didn't think it was going to come off.

Faithful to his word, Michael and his lovely wife Lorraine arrived on a very wet May bank holiday with the granite. How he managed to carry it into the building site I will never know. They sat down to a pile of Welsh cakes and I curiously asked them why they had gone to all this effort for me. They had refused payment for bringing the granite to me from Jersey. Michael simply said that he just knew it wasn't to be cut in two. They had no idea what I wanted it for - maybe a step?

When I shared with them my heart and plans for the house, they were moved to tears. They came in like strangers and went out like best friends! We remain close friends and each time I visit Jersey it always incorporates a time for us to get together with a batch of Welsh cakes for these lovely guys.

The construction of the wall that would house the granite plaque in the orangery was especially designed to take the weight of twelve stone, approximately 2 feet in length and 6 inches in depth.

The big day came when it was being lifted into its housing. It was quite a feat as the underfloor piping had been laid that day and the three men who were needed to carry the heavy granite sculpture had to keep their balance as they manoeuvred between the winding piping.

Everyone was delighted to see this amazing piece of work, beautifully sculptured by Philip Chatfield, at last in its resting place.

The highly-polished cross is central with the symbols of Alpha and Omega each side. There are roughly-carved waves on the lower part with the background carved out to be very rough, signifying our lives before we come to Christ. The design created by Philip was inspired by the cross at Caldey Island near Tenby in west Wales. Philip felt the waves linked the homeland of the stone - Jersey, the inspiration from Caldey Island and the final destination in Swansea near the sea.

It was amazing to see how all the different tradesmen took great interest in the detail we were bringing into this special place and worked very hard with everything they had to do. They were all a joy to have in my somewhat dusty cement-filled home.

It was the summer of 2013 when I finally had my date for my operation, a laparoscopic cholecystectomy - removal of my gall bladder. I had very bad pain for a few years, but managed to control it with a very strict diet, so it was good news that I now had a date to go in. It was a straightforward operation and I was discharged and home within twenty-four hours.

The plasterers were working on the exterior of the house at the time and came filing into the lounge 'to visit' me clutching a beautiful bunch of sunflowers and giving me strict instructions to rest up. It was so funny as every time I got up to do something one of the men would be chastising me and insisting that they were there to look after me between plastering the walls. It was hilarious! Fortunately, I was soon up and about. I paced myself and was soon on the mend.

I am a person who takes pleasure in detail. As I began furnishing the orangery, I knew it had to be practical and very flexible because my intention was that the rooms, rather like a chameleon, had to change very quickly for the different purposes for which they would be used. I needed storage for art equipment and found acacia wooden furniture. During the construction of the tabernacle, acacia wood was one material available to the Israelites. Exodus 35:24 says:

Everyone who had acacia wood for any part of the work brought it.

Acacia wood was used for the poles of the ark, the ark itself, and many parts of the tabernacle. In fact, acacia wood is the only type of wood used in the construction of aspects of the tabernacle.

I thought this would be a great feature for the orangery and was delighted with the large chest and drawer unit. The sofa bed relocated from my upstairs haven and I added a slim-line futon which added to the seating area available.

The pictures on the wall were designed by a dear artist friend, Dawn. Some are originals. One I commissioned her to do which is of the vision the Lord had given me those years before of putting colour back into the lives He sent me to give TLC to.

The dining room furniture was farmhouse pine. A large table that could easily sit eight and ideal for art and craft work. The dresser that I had been given for my first flat fitted perfectly.

The dining room artwork is of a local Jersey artist who uses vibrant colours to depict quirky scenes of the beautiful island in the Channel Isles. Easy chairs completed the furnishings and during winter months the underfloor heating would make it very cosy.

I had planned a big garden party for the completion, but like most builds it ran a little over time so I decided to have a belated firework party towards the end of November. I had invited so many people for the summer party and now that we had delayed it to November, I wondered how we would get everyone in. The kitchen was full of hot cauldrons of soup and Ade's speciality along with copious buffet food and delicious cakes. The guests of all ages arrived - old friends, new friends, and of course the tradesmen who had worked so hard over the months to make this all possible. The house was full to overflowing.

Thank goodness it was a dry night and we were able to spill out into the garden as we had steaming hot non-alcoholic mulled wine served during the firework display. It was a night to remember and Shalom4 was officially birthed.

31

HE WILL DIRECT YOUR PATHS

Trust in the Lord with all your heart and lean not on your own understanding; in all your ways submit to him, and he will make your paths straight (Proverbs 3:5-6 NIV).

It took me a while to adjust to not having my building friends coming each day, but I didn't miss the cement dust and all that goes with building work. During the build I had prayed much for the way in which I was to serve Him in Shalom4. I was clear of my commission to restore weary ladies that He would send me, but totally unsure of the logistics of it all.

Was this to be run like a business? How would I manage on a basic state pension? Was I to charge each guest a fee? How would I advertise? My inner peace felt disturbed and I began to look at my options.

I applied to go on a course for businesses, but knew immediately that this wasn't the way forward. Jackie, a wise counsellor friend of mine, told me of a Christian retreat home in another part of Wales and suggested I talked with them. This was so beneficial and I came home excited and somewhat challenged as I was launching out into the unknown.

The Scripture that I started the chapter with is one that always seems at the forefront in my life when I have to take a big leap of faith. I prayed much about this and found my peace returning when I made a decision to trust God with all that had concerned me. After all He wanted Shalom4 redesigned for His purposes, so surely He had a plan, the best plan of how it would be implemented. Why did I waste time getting myself in knots?

The decision was made. I would not charge my guests. If they chose to give a donation, then I would humbly accept it for the work of Shalom4. I did advertise at the beginning on social media, but soon knew that it wasn't the way forward. He clearly showed me He would be my booking agent and would send those He chose. I was a bit like the innkeeper in the Good Samaritan story (Luke 10:25–37). I felt a huge weight of responsibility lift from my shoulders and began looking forward to my first guests.

I would offer an en-suite guest room with television and tea-making facilities. The stay would be one-to-one, short-term and tailored to their requirements. The house could be freely used by them. Also, I could offer art and craft sessions, and all aspects of spiritual help including prayer. I felt it was important to be able to balance this with my other commitments, particularly my family and time for myself to be refreshed.

My London friends who came for the firework party were my guinea pigs. They were delighted with the guest room and enjoyed their short stay with me. The week after the party, the small art class began on Monday afternoons, twice a month. It was great fun as we tried different arts and crafts together. Often we would have some people who just came for the company. We lit the log fire and served hot chocolate. These were wonderful relaxing afternoons with great company who loved the peace and ambience that they experienced at Shalom4.

The year was coming to a close and what a year it had been, with the fruits of the labour all around me as I thanked God for all the hard work that had been done and for Ade, my builder, who employed the best. It was a work of excellence and I was delighted. My inheritance was spent, all invested into the property. I had so much to be thankful for as I greeted the new year with great anticipation.

I arrived home from Christmas celebrations with my daughter and granddaughter in Jersey with great expectations at what God had in store for me in this new year.

My first guests were Cheryl G from our church, who had completed her master's degree, and her family were coming from Singapore for her graduation and they wanted to spend some time at Shalom4. This was great fun as they wanted to share in the chores and took over the kitchen for the day so that they could produce a fabulous Singaporean 'thank you' meal for all Cheryl's friends she had made whilst in Swansea. What a lovely experience as Shalom4 began its new role. I wanted my guests to feel relaxed and free to use it as their own home and this little family were doing just that. They left with joy and gratefulness in their hearts. What a wonderful start to this new ministry.

A few weeks later my friend Bamidele, another 'adopted daughter', was coming to stay. Let me tell you how I met Bami. It was the first week since my return from Kenya and a grey and rainy summer morning, so different from the vibrancy and colour I had experienced in Africa. I caught the bus to church and was lost in my own thoughts, reflecting on the contrast between my life back home and the lives of those less fortunate than me in Kenya who with the little that they had were still happy and thankful. I was jolted from my thoughts when the bus stopped to pick up four more passengers. A beautiful black lady and her daughter joined us on the bus.

The little girl was brimming with colour in her dress and her wonderful hair with different coloured ribbons adorning it. Her energy matched her colourful attire. She bounced on the bus, promptly sat down and started singing at the top of her voice a song about having Jesus in her heart. Her mum was intently fingering her way through Bible verses - I was elated! This is just what I needed and felt almost transported back to Kenya. I wanted to thank the lady and her little girl, but she alighted the bus before I got chance to speak to her. My spirits lifted and my day was made.

Weeks later I caught the bus to church and at the same stop this lady and her larger-than-life daughter got on the bus. I was delighted and made a beeline over to where they were sitting. I explained how blessed I had been those weeks before and wanted to thank her little girl.

We introduced ourselves and there began a beautiful friendship. Her name was Bami. Her young daughter was called Amy and they had moved from London to Wales because God had told her to! She quickly became my 'bus angel' and often texted me an encouraging word, which was always so timely.

Bami was born in London but spent her formative years from aged two to nineteen in Nigeria. Life had been far from easy. She came to the UK, living with family in London and studied hard achieving her first degree in Economic and Social Policy. Bami's faith was very strong and she had a gift of intercession. She believed God had told her to relocate to Wales to pray for this nation and live among its people. Knowing that all she wanted to do was to obey the prompting of the Holy Spirit, she moved to Swansea with her little toddler Amy. As a single mum she studied hard to achieve her master's in International Development and Human Rights, simultaneously working full-time to support herself and Amy.

Bami was undergoing genetic counselling for breast cancer because of her family history and was advised to have a preventative bilateral mastectomy. This was a very difficult decision and over a period of time she came to the conclusion that this was the way forward for her with reconstruction surgery to take place at the same time as the bilateral mastectomy. Bami had to put weight on as they were using her own tummy tissue for reconstruction. One big operation and further operations to follow.

Bami made arrangements with me to come to Shalom4 for TLC and convalescing following her twelve-and-a-half-hour operation.

Bami arrived on a cold February Monday afternoon following her operation. She gingerly walked to the corner of the lounge and took possession of the recliner chair. I wrapped her in a warm fluffy blanket and got a hot drink for her as she settled and dozed. It happened to be the art afternoon, so my ladies worked on the dining room table 'quietly', continuing with their creations. It wasn't long before Bami was wide awake and talking and praying with them. Nothing kept this lady down!

It was a privilege to serve Bami in this way and see Shalom4 being used for His purposes of giving love and TLC to all those He sent to me. Bami's decision to have such drastic surgery wasn't taken lightly by her. There was much agonising and prayer. It was a huge shock to her and her surgeon when the histology results came back. The tests showed invasive DCIS which is Stage 1 breast cancer. Her decision to have the preventative operation proved to have been the wisest decision she had ever made.

Though the following few years were not easy, with more operations and coming to terms with so much, Bami pressed on and qualified as a life coach. Her passion for writing led her to record her amazing story in *Navigating Your New Normal* to help others who find their lives crumble with the trauma that life can bring.

I'm so very proud of this young lady who is sold out for God, who perseveres and always comes through so powerfully. She and Amy have a future and a hope and the best is yet to come!

32

DANCING IN THE RAIN

This chapter heading might seem very strange to you; read on and you will find out why.

I want to tell you about Dawn. I first met Dawn many years ago at church. Naïvely I thought artists were flamboyant, eccentric, zany and somewhat quirky. This wasn't Dawn; she was a quiet, thoughtful and elegant lady, not a bit like my artist-type impression.

I learnt Dawn was a trained teacher and later became a tutor, teaching pupils who could not go to school for some reason or other. Dawn had a degree in graphic design and product design, but art was her passion and she had her own unique style which I loved.

One day as I was in the middle of the alterations at Shalom4, my lovely friend Dawn arrived to talk about the forthcoming craft fair where she would exhibit her prophetic art. Dawn had been inspired by the Christian conference, Spring Harvest. They encouraged artists to create through the medium of paint during church meetings and depict what God was saying to them.

Dawn returned and in church services began to draw what God was saying to her during the sermons. Her prophetic art was birthed and we were very excited about launching her new artwork to the public. We met up frequently to discuss planning and schedules for her to exhibit and sell her work.

One morning Dawn came to Shalom4 and told me she had found a breast lump. She wasn't particularly concerned and said she'd make an appointment soon to see her GP. Outwardly I looked calm, cool and collected, but inside I felt worried for her. She saw her GP straightaway and an urgent referral was made to the Breast Care Clinic. Tests were done and the bombshell dropped: Dawn had a diagnosis of breast cancer. She would need a lumpectomy.

We have a special bonding and I thanked God for that. Her husband would be supporting her through whatever was ahead. She also gave me the privilege of being a strong arm for her to lean on whenever she needed me and of course the shelter of Shalom4.

After the operation for a second lumpectomy, Dawn was surprised at her follow-up appointment that she would need chemotherapy and radiotherapy to make sure all was clear. I had a suspicion that this would be the case, but knew that news was broken in stages so that a person isn't overwhelmed.

The after-effects of the treatment made Dawn exhausted and without energy. Shalom4 became her regular haven to rest and receive TLC during these times. I felt so privileged to be able to support her in this way.

We couldn't understand why this had happened just as she was launching her new art business, but we trusted God that He would bring good out of even this. Her hair was falling out so the wig we had shopped for a few weeks earlier was timely for her to use. She still looked the same lovely Dawn.

Ironically, at the same time of Dawn's treatment, my young friend Cath had a similar diagnosis. Cath however needed a bilateral mastectomy with treatment to follow. Dawn and Cath met for the first time at Shalom4 and shared experiences of their cancer journey as they sat with steaming-hot, home-made soup and rolls in their new glamorous wigs and a stoic determination that the cancer wasn't going to beat them. What an inspiration these lovely ladies were.

After some months Dawn recovered with a new zest for life and with an all-clear result. Her mortality had been threatened but she was determined to live each day to the full. She had a renewed vigour for her art work and went from strength to strength in confidence. Dawn's work is now in south and west Wales in various shops and galleries, and she exhibits in the local arts and crafts fairs.

During this time, Dawn and Cath attended workshops organised by various cancer charities and one of the amazing things Dawn produced was a scrapbook of her breast cancer journey. They were so impressed with it that it led to her being asked to speak in Cardiff at the launch of Cancer Research Wales.

What an example these courageous ladies have been to so many. They faced their traumatic diagnosis of breast cancer; they got through the unpleasant and exhausting treatments and turned their health issues into a positive result, proving that God brings good even out of the most devastating situations that life can throw at us.

Their faith in God, who cares for every detail of their lives, made them victorious. Both to this day are doing well and enjoying life as never before.

Did they allow their diagnosis to determine who they were? Certainly not; they faced it head on.

Although some days were more difficult than others, they came through.

The key was that they put all their trust in God and knew that whatever the outcome, they were safe in His arms. They could dance...even in the rain!

Individuals who have learned to endure and persevere through the storms of hardships are those who can dance in the rain during a storm (Ellen J. Barrier).

I continued to enjoy a steady stream of weary ladies who frequented Shalom4. The guest book is filled with encouraging remarks of their time spent there. They were welcomed with open arms and I was able to pour His love and TLC into each lady who came. To see them leaving refreshed and recharged was such a reward and confirmation that I was doing His will.

33

END OF AN ERA

Aunty Betty's health issues were on a steady decline. She had been regularly falling and needing hospitalisation over the months. She had carers coming in daily and they were increased to the maximum of four a day. I continued to oversee her, visiting her and co-ordinating her needs, but was still able to continue with the work at Shalom4, as well as my hospital volunteering and regular visits to family in Jersey.

As the months passed, Aunty Betty became more and more unwell. Her fall in the new year made it impossible for her to continue living on her own any longer. She asked if I would get her into Hengoed Court Care Home, a nursing home near her own home.

I visited the home and was very impressed with the bright and cheerful decor, pleasant outlook with sea views and the light and airy individual rooms that each resident had to make their own.

We were very fortunate that there was a room available and she was taken from her hospital bed to her new home. I personalised her room with her treasured framed photographs and ornaments that were precious to her. I made a string of bunting from some of her old familiar material she had given me. She arrived delighted at my efforts but with much fear and tribulation at the thought of not being able to be independent any longer and of course leaving her beloved home. We hear of ailing folks daily having to leave their homes and lose their independence, but until we ourselves experience it we cannot fully understand the sadness and grief that it must bring.

Her fears were unfounded and she began to settle into her new surroundings, although insisted that she would stay in her own room and not venture forth to join other residents. Her mobility was not good following her last fall and her needing a hip replacement. The staff were wonderful, jolly, kind and thoughtful. I joked with them that I certainly would like to live there if I couldn't look after myself, and I meant it too!

Aunty Betty asked me to sell her bungalow. I had spent time while she was in hospital redecorating it and making it ready for the inevitable sale. It was a blessing that it sold very quickly.

She had only been there just over a month when she became very unwell. It was distressing to see her and she sadly passed away. The end of an era and a life that had served the Lord.

For many years Betty had been housebound and had to rely on others. She was a strong character, very much like her sibling, my dad. There are many stories that could be fondly told of her, but probably the best would be her generosity, especially to the children who came into her life which left lasting good memories. It wasn't always easy for me, but I remember all her kindness and love that she gave to so many over the years.

Some months later when all the family were able to be together from various parts of the globe, we followed her strict instructions to have her ashes interred in an old family grave in Abergavenny. Here she had happy childhood memories. It was a special day as we gathered together and thanked God for her life.

I want to thank Tony Daniels, a very distant cousin for all his input in Aunty Betty's life. I couldn't have done it without him. There were times when I was at the end of my tether, but Tony hung in there with me and sometimes for me. Her church was Lonlas Mission and Jim Webber and Richard Jenkins, as well as the wider congregation, journeyed with her over many years. I am eternally grateful and thankful to God for having met them through their involvement with Betty.

Betty will never be forgotten by all the family and those lives she touched over many decades in her life. She is at peace with God; hallelujah!

34

CHAPLAINCY AND HOSPICE WORK

Even though I walk through the darkest valley, I will fear no evil, for you are with me (Psalm 23:4, NIV).

One of the highlights of my week for many years has been my work as a volunteer in hospitals and hospice. It started over thirty years ago when I used to take a sweet trolley around the wards of a little cottage hospital in Clydach. I loved meeting the patients and having the time to listen to each person. Staff in hospitals are often overworked and sadly may not have the time.

One particular day I noticed a gentleman who was recovering from a stroke. He had lost the use of one side of his body, his speech was slurred, he was hard to understand, and he cried a lot. My heart went out to him. His wife had died, he didn't see his son often and it looked as if he would not be able to return to his home.

I sat with him week after week giving him time to express himself through his often-incomprehensible speech. Soon I won his trust. He looked forward to my visits and through his tears he began to smile, even if it was lopsided. He had been in hospital for a long time and they felt he had come to the capacity of recovery, leaving him paralysed down one side of his body.

His situation was heavy on my heart and I prayed daily for him. During one of these prayer times I felt God asking me to pray over him. I was to lay my hands appropriately on his paralysed side and ask God to heal

211

him. This was all new to me at the time, but I wanted to be obedient to what God had said.

On my next visit with my sweet trolley, as I was sitting with him, I asked if I could pray over him. He looked surprised and a bit cynical, but agreed anyway.

We knew that the physiotherapists had felt that he had reached his capacity following his stroke those months earlier. I quietly began to pray for him, laying my hands, with his permission, onto his paralysed side. The prayer was simple as I asked God to heal him. Nothing physically happened, no fireworks, but simply praying what I believe God had asked. I left shortly afterwards leaving the result to the Lord; after all, this was His plan.

I arrived a week later equipped with a squeezy stress ball that I thought I could work with on his paralysed hand. I started to explain what I had thought to do when he shook his head, uttering very secretively beside his bed and began to tell me what had happened.

Not long after we had prayed the week before he began to feel pins and needles in his hands and feet. He hadn't told the staff as he felt they wouldn't believe him. Each day he concentrated on his feet and hands and very slowly he began to move them.

Eventually he told the medics who were astonished and physiotherapy began again. God had begun an amazing healing. How we praised Him for His goodness and love!

He was moved to a residential home where I continued to visit him. The best visit ever was arriving one day to find him up on a Zimmer frame with the physiotherapist beaming as he had walked the length of the corridor - his first steps since he had the stroke those months before. Oh, how we rejoiced that day!

Then there was Gwyn. I met Gwyn in Clydach Cottage Hospital. He was a young man cut off in the prime of his life when riding his beloved motorbike. He had a stroke that left him severely disabled, immobile and without speech. He laughed and cried a lot. He was such a patient, determined young man. He had lost the control of the saliva in his mouth and would drool uncontrollably.

I remember one of the biggest challenges of my life was when I had got him an ice cream and was helping him eat it. He motioned for me to have a lick of his ice cream. I have a real problem with sharing food, so I found myself freeze and send a silent 'help' prayer up because the last thing I wanted to do was to offend this dear man. I took a deep breath and took the tiniest lick of the ice cream and managed to cope, but only just!

Gwyn, as I mentioned in an earlier chapter, came to my baptism. He made such an effort as friends hauled his wheelchair up and down the steep steps at the beach. There was one occasion when my kindness stretched too far! We were serving drinks and Gwyn wanted a drink of fruit cordial. I poured a tumbler full for him and passed it to him. The next minute the poor man was nearly choking to death. He had taken a huge swig and unknown to me, it had been neat, undiluted cordial! The poor man was as red as a beetroot and gasping for breath. I hasten to add he recovered very quickly, much to our relief.

Then there was Alan, Judy's brother. He had had a

heart and lung transplant. The operation was successful. He was in the high dependency unit with all its machines and strange sounds. It was Alan's birthday; I had made him a cake and took it into the ward. He was awake but unable to speak because he was wired to a breathing machine. I carried the cake into the ward, expecting him to be delighted that I had remembered.

As I drew closer, his eyes became larger and larger, almost fearful. He started to gesture towards the cake and was shaking his head. I was just about to light the candles when I remembered about the piped oxygen throughout the ward and realised that Alan was trying to warn me not to light the candles!

Oxygen and naked flame aren't a good combination. The relief on his face when he knew I put the matches away was something else! You would have thought I wouldn't have been let loose near the hospital after all my escapades; perhaps it was a good thing I didn't put them on my application forms!

I think the times at Clydach Cottage Hospital gave me the impetus to take on the challenge of volunteering in Tŷ Olwen hospice. I enjoyed the interaction with patients and staff and loved the camaraderie amongst all those who worked there. As I worked among the sick and the dying, I saw compassion demonstrated in the most loving and caring ways.

We realised that we weren't there to evangelise but knew that we could silently take Jesus in with us to shine His light into the darkness of sickness and death. On some occasions we would have an opportunity to share our faith when the patient asked us. This was always a great privilege for us.

I remember Cyril. He was a very large man with a terminal prognosis. He was of gypsy stock and had a chequered past. He drew my attention to a leaflet on his locker. It was a forthcoming Christian rally that he wanted to be well enough to attend. I sat beside him and listened intently as he shared with tears pouring onto the bed sheets. He had found the Lord years before but had taken paths away from God and was full of regret and remorse. He sobbed as he shared what he had done and wanted to go to the rally to repent and find his peace with God again.

When he had finished talking, I gently assured him that he didn't need to get to the rally but could repent and find his peace with God from the very bed he was in. His eyes widened and said he had to be on his knees before God to repent and say sorry. He heaved his fluid-filled body onto the floor, oblivious of anyone or anything going on in the ward around him. He knelt almost prostrate before God and repented, sobbing uncontrollably. Then he stopped. The torment had left his face and was replaced with the peace that passes all understanding.

He had his joy back as he had reconciled himself with his Saviour. I helped him back into his bed, still in awe of what had happened and thankful that we had actually had the ward to ourselves during those precious moments.

God had most certainly engineered the space and the time. Together we rejoiced and marvelled at what He had done!

The twelve years were life-changing for me. The privilege to be alongside the sick and the dying for me was like fulfilling the vision that I had from God. Many times we had the opportunity to share the love of Jesus with the patients. We knew we had to be discreet, but when they wanted to talk about their mortality and faith, we were able to comfort them spiritually also.

The hospice was undergoing a refurbishment and relocated to a part of the Oncology Ward at Singleton Hospital. I could see how the main ward could benefit from having volunteers. Providentially, a course became available to train chaplaincy lay visitors. This would mean I could be part of the team serving Wards 11 and 12 Oncology and Haematology. I completed the course and took up my new role.

It was thrilling to be able to serve God in this way. I loved the freedom to be able to spend as much or as little time with the patients as they wanted. The staff welcomed me into this role and I soon became part of the team in the ward.

About six months later as I entered the ward, a staff nurse came up to me and asked if I felt I could help them. Sadie (nom de plume) was in the side ward and had terminal cancer.

She had a terrible night and needed a member of staff to stay with her all the time. She was very scared and in a real state of fear. I entered her room to find her pinned up against the bedhead, petrified with fear. She went on to explain that she felt there was something horrible in the room. Although I was not personally aware of a presence, I knew she was. I asked her if she wanted it to go and said that the only way I knew that would definitely work was to ask Jesus to take it away. I sat beside her, reassuring her and began to pray a simple prayer asking Jesus to clear the room of anything that was evil. Immediately I finished she gave a deep sigh and relaxed completely. Fear had completely left her face. 'It's gone. How did you do that?'

I explained that it wasn't me, but the power of Jesus. 'I want what you've got,' she said hastily. I explained to her the way to salvation in Jesus and left her relaxed and at peace as she reflected on all I shared. Never let us underestimate the power of the Name of Jesus.

The following week I visited her during my ward round. She was delighted to see me and excitedly told me that she had asked Jesus to come into her heart. I was overjoyed to see Sadie and despite her terminal cancer, she was serene in her demeanour. Eager to know more, she asked for a Bible and a daily reading book which I supplied for her. She had a spiritual hunger despite feeling so ill.

I didn't see Sadie over the next few weeks as she had been discharged and had gone home to her husband and young son. Later that month she was readmitted. Her breathing wasn't good and she relied on oxygen for part of the day. She told me how tired she felt, but kept going for her husband and her son's sake. She improved a little and was discharged.

A month or so after this I went into the ward. I must confess I was very tired and went around most rooms, but decided that I would leave a little earlier and catch up on some rest. I turned to leave the ward and that inner voice of the Holy Spirit that had so often spoken to me to guide me, spoke again; I heard, 'Go back,' and again, 'Go back.' So not wanting to disobey, I turned on my heels, retraced my steps and into the ward that I had missed out.

There was Sadie, hooked up to the oxygen, beckoning me to come to her bedside. She wanted to know how I knew she wanted to speak to me. I told her I didn't, but God obviously did! Sadie told me that she could no longer fight; she was exhausted and wanted to go home to Jesus and heaven. She was adamant. Despite knowing that she had kept going thus far for the sake of her husband and son, she was ready. I asked her if she wanted me to pray that God would take her? A big 'yes' was her reply.

I took Sadie in my arms and she drew into the contours of my body. I could feel every bone as the cancer had reduced her to skin and bone. She tucked her head against mine and whispered her thanks to me, and I prayed very simply that God would hear her prayer and that Jesus would take her home.

We hugged one another and said our goodbyes. She asked me to get one of the chaplains to take her communion, which I duly arranged for the next morning. When the chaplain went in to take her communion as arranged, he was told that she had passed away the afternoon before. I was so surprised so I asked the staff when I next visited what had happened. They explained that after I left, they went to serve lunch and she refused it saying she didn't need it as she was going to heaven! Sadie went into a deep sleep and never woke up.

Once again God had honoured her wishes that we prayed for. The staff were shocked as there were no warning signs of imminent death.

God's ways are not our ways. For Sadie, he had delivered her from fear those months earlier. She now had no fear and was filled with blessed assurance as she peacefully slipped into the arms of Jesus. What a wonderful way for her to leave this earth.

Sadie taught me a lot. We can so complicate our faith when he wants us to remain like little children. Simply believe and trust.

Over the years I have met many who have come through the wards. Some didn't make it; some are still out there living a life with quality, thanks to the dedication of the oncology multidisciplinary team - the doctors, nurses and staff connected with this amazing work, as well as the chemotherapy and radiotherapy departments and those dedicated in the community. Each person plays a vital part in the lives of those challenged with cancer.

After I had been in chaplaincy and on the ward for over six years, an opportunity and opening became available for me to work in Tŷ Olwen hospice again with a dear friend called Helen, who was part of the chaplaincy team. I was delighted that I could do both oncology and hospice work.

I love the ethos of the hospice and since being back there nearly two years, it is the highlight of my week. The input we have with patients, families and friends is amazing. Their gratitude to all at the hospice is such a source of encouragement. I'm often asked if it's a sad place. They are shocked when I say it's often a place of joy! It's a place of safety and support for each patient and their family and friends. Life isn't always about 'quantity, but quality', and that's what they do so well.

Over the last years Helen, my dear friend and fellow volunteer, and I are privileged to be part of staff support alongside talking with patients, families and friends.

Chaplaincy support helps them to know we are there for them to encourage and comfort them when they need it. Hospice work is vocational and in my experience the staff are handpicked.

The compassion and care are second-to-none. It's inevitable that tears are often shed by the staff as they give their all to care for each individual patient.

We see God's presence in and through their work and our hope is that the chaplaincy team's presence in their workplace will continue to bring them comfort and hope to carry on their dedicated work with palliative patients.

We have had the privilege of instigating the restoration of the recently-renovated garden room situated in the grounds of Tŷ Olwen, which is now proving to be a sanctuary for the staff as a place to be still and reflect during difficult times.

35

CAROL

This book of shared experiences with wonderful people God has brought into my life would not be complete without sharing Carol with you. I briefly told you in an earlier chapter a little about how we met during the trying times of my life as Dad's carer.

After our initial meeting, we knew that we were enriching each other's lives in a special way. Dad for some reason affectionately nicknamed her Olga! So, Olga she was to me too and I became Ida to her as she claimed I was skilled at allowing problems to wash over me, rather like water off an 'eider' duck's back.

Carol is a talented lady. She speaks Welsh fluently, plays the harp beautifully and tickles the keys of a piano melodiously. More than that, she has one of the biggest hearts. Carol responds to needs instantly and sacrificially. To add to that, she is so much fun. I loved these qualities about her straight away.

She is zany and quirky and certainly not boring - absolutely my type of person! We knew God had brought us together and were excited to see what was ahead. We supported one another in our caring roles for our ailing parents and were there for one another when their lives came to an end.

When I was away and Dad was in respite, Carol took her harp into Rose Cross House and entertained him and the other residents. What a concert they had! I can see her now kneeling affectionately beside Dad, talking gently to him to encourage and settle him, kindness pouring from her. We were a force to be reckoned with when we were together. Nothing was too hot for us.

Let me tell you a couple of stories. Carol had decided to take up an appeal for clothes for Iraq. She had put her request on social media and alerted friends. A small team of willing volunteers assembled at Greenfields Church in Morriston to begin to collect and sort any clothes that might come in. Before we knew it, the black bags became like a mountain. As fast as we were sorting them, more were coming. I had never seen so many clothes!

Every time we heard the sound of a car arriving in the car park, we would groan with horror at the thought of more clothes to sort out. But we would greet the kind contributors with a grateful smile and occasional hug.

At one stage, to keep us sane, we decided to have a dress-up time. It was hilarious and we all fell about in hysterical laughter, which in some strange way energised us to plough through the mountains of clothes.

By the second day we were all completely exhausted but thoroughly rewarded as we completed our task. We all agreed we didn't want to see any more bulging black bags of clothes for a very long time!

Some months later, I had a call from Carol. It was a prayer request. A dear friend, Chris, had fallen down the stairs in his home he shared with his mother. When he was scanned, they discovered a terminal brain tumour. He was working as a porter in the local hospital as well as caring for his aged mother, who was devastated as were his many friends and colleagues.

His mum was unable to manage on her own any longer and was taken to a nursing home. Chris was moved to the hospice for a short time. The tumour had the effect of a stroke on his body and within the space of a few short months, he was in need of full-time care. Fortunately, he was able to be moved to the same nursing home as his mum, which meant they could still see one another each day.

Carol offered to help sort the house they rented. When I heard this, I offered to help her and we worked solidly for months. This was quite a challenge as there was a lot to do. Those who know me are aware how I love doing this sort of thing. Despite the sad situation, we *did* have some funny times! When we were sorting out the many black bags of unwanted paperwork and items that they no longer wanted or needed, we recognised that we needed help in disposing of them.

Carol looked on social media and found an advert for shed and house clearance, etc. Delighted with her find, she arranged a time for collection. The two young men arrived, but no van, just a small Ford Fiesta. They told us that their van had broken down. They were adamant they could do the job and filled the car to overflowing with broken furniture and other bulky items which took them a number of trips.

Ford would have been proud to use these guys as an advert for the Fiesta. No one else could have crammed as much stuff into one car as these guys did. It's an art to fold a double mattress into four! Carol happily paid them and they drove away. It was a great feeling and we began to see a big dent in our work of clearing out the house.

Some days later, a neighbour called Carol. To her horror the police had been knocking her door. They had found confidential papers and thought the house had been burgled!

The young men were not legitimate and had simply dumped the paper at the edge of some farm and tried to set the bags alight. We were in shock. They were looking for quick drug money. We wondered if they had stolen the car to collect the rubbish.

It taught us a lesson not to trust every advertisement you read. We were grateful that we weren't arrested for illegal disposing of confidential mail! Never a dull moment with Carol, and I look forward with anticipation to the next time I get a call from her. I never stop thanking God for her.

Over the last few years, I have seen this lovely friend face a diagnosis of lymphoma and watched her face her future so victoriously through hospital appointments, chemotherapy and other drug therapies.

Carol remained positive, still ministering to those whom she met on her journey with a smile, an encouraging word, and always filling herself with the needs of others and never focused on her own health issues.

She was an inspiration to all who met her. Sadly, she left us for heaven in September 2019. She is missed by many. I can only say that for me a colour went out of my life.

At the service of celebration of her life, a friend and colleague who spoke shared her accomplishments as a teacher and musician, and reminded us that when a performance is exceptional the audience gives a standing ovation. He invited us, a church full to the brim of those who loved her, to give her a standing ovation. It was one of the most moving experiences. Everyone stood and clapped until our hands tingled.

Carol Harris, heaven is a richer place with you there and we are sure you will be playing your harp for Jesus. Thank you for the privilege of knowing you, precious friend.

36

LOCKDOWN
FACING A NEW NORMAL

This final chapter is written at a time I thought I would never experience in my lifetime. As I came into the new year of 2020, I began making travel plans. Trips were booked for Jersey so I could help my daughter during her working hours. A holiday was booked for Zante in Greece and countless weekly commitments filled up my calendar for the year…or so I thought!

News began filtering through of a new virus called Coronavirus or Covid-19, beginning in China. People were dying from it. With lightning speed it began to spread through Europe and many nations. It hit the UK and by late March the country was placed in lockdown. We were told it would hit the elderly and the vulnerable with health issues, but we soon learnt that this virus had a mind of its own and was affecting every age group: a silent killer.

As I write, the UK is seven weeks into lockdown with a very uncertain future. Nobody really knows at this stage which way it is going to go. The reality is that until a vaccine can be developed, nobody is really safe. No amount of social distancing will keep everyone completely safe as this is a war with an unseen enemy. It can linger on surfaces, such as fabric, metal, plastic.

One thing is certain: God is still in control and will use this unprecedented time to turn it to good. A quotation from Amy Carmichael said, 'In acceptance lieth peace.' This is so right. We need time to process the changes we are experiencing at this moment, but as we begin to accept the things we cannot change, then a peace is brought to us. We need to begin to navigate our 'new normal'.

For those of us who know Jesus as our personal Saviour, there is a hope fixed deeply in the core of our being. I know that He is walking alongside me just as He has in the stories I have shared with you in this book. He is unshakeable. Whatever the outcome, we have the hope of eternal life with Him. My times are in His hands.

I felt prompted by Him to 'trim my lamp'; this means to be ready for His return. I know that God's time isn't limited to our concept of time. One day to Him may be a thousand years to us…and vice versa. I am learning to be obedient to what He says and I'm trimming my lamp during this period of enforced stay-at-home time.

This book is something He asked me to write, to tell of His wonders. I hope that you have seen something in these pages of a loving God who delights in His children. He is a protective and just God. If our path has suffering along its way, He promises us that He will be beside us every step of the way.

I pray for you, dear reader, that if you don't already know Jesus as your personal Saviour, that the reality of God's love and forgiveness will envelope you.

So, whatever the outcome of Covid-19 on my life, self-isolating, social-distancing for months or even years, whether it passes me by, gives me mild symptoms or takes my life, I have utter peace that I am safe in the arms of Jesus, and through the help of others have managed to complete my story thus far.

Who knows there could even be a sequel…

I pray that you have been blessed, challenged and brought nearer to finding Jesus in your own life and been taken into a deeper relationship with Him as you have read just a few of His awesome and wondrous ways. He intervenes in our lives when we ask Him to come and live within us.

If you want to accept Jesus as your Saviour, reflect on the following prayer and pray it from your heart. He will come to you…

Lord Jesus, the things I have read in this book about You makes me want to know You for myself. I come to You today and open my heart to You. I confess my sins to You and ask you to forgive me and come and live in my heart. I want You to take over my life and make me new. Thank You that You say in the Bible that You turn no one away who comes to You and You promise that from that second, I enter eternal life. Take over my life, Lord Jesus. Amen.

If you have prayed that prayer, contact someone you know who is a committed Christian to help you on your journey. I promise you that this will be the best decision you have made in your life.

I conclude with a word from the Preface: '…you will never be the same…'

To God be the glory, great things he has done.

Printed in Great Britain
by Amazon

44893474R00136